Tracing Your Family Tree

Tracing Your Family Tree

The Complete Guide to Discovering your Family History

Jean A. Cole and Michael Armstrong

GUILD PUBLISHING LONDON

To Mary Armstrong and Reg Cole who have shown great patience, tolerance and understanding and for their help throughout the writing of this book.

This edition published 1988
by Guild Publishing
by arrangement with Thorsons Publishing Group.

Printed in Great Britain

Contents

Acknowledgements

The authors would like to thank all those who kindly gave permission to use illustrations and photographs from parish, diocesan and individual collections in this book and for help and assistance received.

The Revd Peter J. Shepherd, Vicar of Yaxley, Cambs., and Yaxley Church Council: Canon W.M. Debney, F.C.A., Rector of Brampton, Cambs.: The Venerable Richard Sledge, Archdeacon of Huntingdon: The Revd D.H.G. Clark, Vicar of Godmanchester, Cambs.: The Revd Mark G. Goodhand, Methodist Minister of St. Ives, Cambs.: Mr Alex Hill and the staff of Cambridgeshire County Record Office (Huntingdon Branch): The Deputy Chief Constable of Cambridgeshire County Constabulary Headquarters, Cambridge: The Wiltshire Record Office, Trowbridge: The Wiltshire Archaeological and Natural History Museum, Devizes: Dr. John Chandler of the Wiltshire Record Society: The Gloucestershire Record Office and Tetbury feoffees: The Devon Record Office, Exeter: The Church of Jesus Christ of Latter Day Saints, London: Mr D.M. Allen, Divisional Library, Swindon, Wilts.: The Hon. John Montagu: Capt. J.W.H. Goddard of Rendcomb, Cirencester: Mrs Shirley Lancaster of Thornhill, Ontario, Canada: Mr Francis Leeson: Crown Copyright Records by permission of the Controller of H.M. Stationery Office.

Mrs Sue Avory who assisted with much of the typing of the manuscript. Mr Brian Christmas for proof-reading and genealogical observations.

Introduction

The reasons why people set out on the family history trail are many and varied. For some, family stories, handed down through the generations, act as a trigger. For others, an old photograph, or perhaps an ancestral diary, or family bible; with others it is simply curiosity. The subject fascinates people from all walks of life. We can be as different from one another as chalk from cheese, but yet we have this one common, all-absorbing need to find when and how our ancestors lived.

The long term aim is to find out everything possible about them. After all, it is our forbears who have handed down the physical and mental characteristics which have made us as we are today. Perhaps there is a history of twins in the family, or a talent for painting, needlework or some other skill which may have come down through the generations. Tracing your family history could help you discover from which family line these traits have arisen.

It is essential to realize that most families have, over the years, had their 'ups and downs', ranging from yeoman stock to landed gentry, or from labourers to tradesmen or members of a profession. Some forbears will have been hardworking members of the community, both outgoing and cheerful; some maybe were reserved or taciturn, whilst others were sickly, and feckless; perhaps a few were even capable of breaking the law. You could discover ancestors in gaol or the poor-house; others will have been churchwardens, lawyers or even magistrates. Time and circumstances may have often changed the lifestyle of the family, the rich becoming poor, and the poor becoming rich. All of your ancestors will have handed down some of their characteristics which make you the way you look, think, talk, walk, and act.

The art of tracing the history of any family lies in the researcher's ability to find, read, and copy the appropriate records in a perspicuous manner. Nowadays, from birth to death the average person leaves behind a trail of official and unofficial clues to where and how they have spent their life. This trail can start off even before birth with pre-natal records, but the first most important record in a person's life is, of course, his or her birth certificate. From this we learn where a person was born, the names of the parents, the maiden name of the mother, and the occupation of the father. This gives a researcher a whole lot of clues with which to step back to a previous generation.

Later on in life, the person is perhaps baptized, and here again a further clue is left behind for future generations as the event is recorded. Then come records from such events as school, marriage, children, work, union membership, retirement, pensions, and ultimately death, with perhaps, publication of a will, or letters of administration if the person dies intestate (leaving no will). To add to these, there are a host of other possibilities, such as business accounts, invoices, family bibles, diaries, photographs and newspaper

This excellent illustration of the sources to use when tracing your family tree was composed by 14 year old J.P. Bloore of Hagley, West Midlands.

cuttings, divorce, apprenticeship, criminal files, armed service or merchant/naval records. To list all the possibilities here would be impossible.

Tracing family history is one of those hobbies in which old leads eventually peter out, only to be replaced by a whole new set of exciting possibilities. Without doubt, it is one of the most fascinating pastimes around. Many of our ancestors led such eventful lives that it seems wrong to leave their stories hidden in archives. Here follows a short compilation of extracts from an excellent article which appeared in *Family Tree Magazine* (Vol. 2, No. 2, January 1986). The article was called 'Farrier Major Avison' and it was sent in by a reader, one Richard Wormald. It vividly illustrates the way in which it is possible to build up a life story mainly from one source of records.

Those who have not had the occasion, or who have not found it possible for one reason or another, to search the Public Record Office at Kew for information about their military forebears or relations can have little idea how rewarding such a search may prove.

The biographical information gleaned may be considerable and, at best, it is possible to reconstruct the whole service life of the officer or soldier whom one is researching.

Born in March 1809 at Thornhills by Dewsbury, Charles Avison was christened on April 23, 1809 in the ancient church of St Peter, Hartshead, where his father, Samuel, a farmer of Thornhills, was churchwarden.

Charles, the fourth surviving son of his family, must have been apprenticed to a smith and farrier; his service records state this as his trade on enlistment.

He enlisted in the 11th Light Dragoons at Leeds, and was attested there for the Regiment on May 22, 1830, recruited most likely by a detachment of the Regiment sent to the North of England specifically as a recruiting party.

His attestation papers state his age on enlistment as 21 years two months, and his birthplace as 'in or near Dewsbury in the County of York'. His height was given as precisely five feet and three eighth inches. He was fresh complexioned, with grey eyes and dark brown hair.

The 11th Light Dragoons had been serving in India, 'East India' as it was then called, for 11 years when Charles enlisted, and it is in the Muster Rolls of the single troop of the Regiment stationed at the Cavalry Depot at Maidstone Barracks, Kent, that '644 Pte Avison, Charles' begins to appear, following his enlistment.

Charles was stationed at Maidstone until shown 'embarked on 5th March 1831'. He was, of course, on his way to join his Regiment in India.

From the Army Chaplain's Returns of Marriages for that period, at present held at the General Register Office, St Catherine's House, London, we learn that on August 10, 1836 in the last year that the Regiment was stationed at Meerut, Charles married an Elizabeth Hard. Later, the 1841 and 1851 Censuses for England show Charles' bride to have been aged 16, and born at Downpatrick in Ireland.

Curiously enough, it is from the marriage entry that we see Charles' army role stated for the first time as 'farrier'. On December 4 and 11, 1837, the 11th left Cawnpore, embarking two divisions and sailing down the Ganges to Calcutta. The Muster Rolls show them successively at Bankipore, Balou Ghat and Calcutta. Charles is with the second division (under Major Rotton), which embarked at Calcutta on February 2, 1838, the entry being 'Sea, on the Battleship the Repulse'. They were 'on board ship 145 days', and 'landed at Gravesend on June 25, 1838', disembarking the following day, and proceeding to Canterbury.

It was at Canterbury, on June 13 1839 that Charles and Elizabeth's second son Samuel was born. The certificate states that at half past 9 pm at the Artillery barracks, Charles is described as 'Farrier Major in the 11th Light Dragoons' although he remains listed in the Muster Rolls simply as Private. Not long after Charles' return to duty on January 20, 1840 it must have become known that the 11th had been chosen to meet Prince Albert of Saxe-Coburg at Dover and escort him to London for his marriage to Queen Victoria. The Prince arrived at Dover on February 7, 1840 and was escorted to Canterbury and from there, on the following day, to the Palace.

Little then appears from the Muster Rolls until 1854, when the Rolls for the second quarter, ended June 30, are dated from Turkey, and show the 11th to have been 50 days on board ship. They are about to take part in the Crimean War.

A contemporary account tells us that the 11th had been warned on March 9, 1854 that they were bound for foreign service; and they had sailed from Kingstown Harbour on May 10 in five transports 'hired' to take them East. Women, on a basis of four per troop, had been permitted. It would seem obvious that Charles' wife, Elizabeth, with three young sons, would remain behind.

On arriving in Turkey, they took up position at Varna as part of the Light Brigade. At the end of August, the Muster Rolls show them on board ship, embarked for the Crimea. There, the intention of the British and their main allies, the French, was to defeat the enemy, the Russians, and take the fortress of Sebastopol.

The Battle of Alma which was fought on September 20, followed on October 25 by the Battle of Balaclava. It was in the course of this battle that the Light Brigade, with the Earl of Cardigan at their head, made their famous charge down the 'valley of death' into the Russian guns.

At the Royal Hussars Museum, at Winchester, are some small flowers sent from the Crimea by Charles Avison. The note enclosing them reads:

'These flowers were gathered from the spot where many of our brave heroes fell in the cavalry charge of Balaclava. C. Avison, Farrier Major'.

After the storm of November 14 came snow and the bitter Crimean winter. Supply arrangements were chaotic, with no provision for suitable clothing against the cold for the troops and no fodder for the cavalry horses, which were literally starving to death. Hospital arrangements for the sick and wounded had not had time to respond to the efforts of the newly-arrived Florence Nightingale and were still appalling.

The next reference to Charles is a note against his name showing him to have been 'invalided to England' on June 11 1855. Just before leaving the Crimea, Charles wrote to Elizabeth. The letter, now with the Royal Hussars Museum, is headed 'Camp Nr Balaclava. June 8th 1855.' Charles writes that he is 'expecting every day the order to embark on board ship'.

Referring to the previous day's attack on the enemy's batteries to capture part of their works at Sebastopol, he writes of the, for him, unforgettable sight of the brave men who 'raised the British cheer' as they advanced to victory into the smoke of the enemy's guns, many never to return.

Charles receives one more mention in the Muster Rolls when, on the appointment in October 1855 of a John Dyke as Farrier Major, it is stated that Charles had been discharged at Chatham. Charles' discharge documents at Kew show that he arrived in the UK on August 8 1855. On August 12 he appeared before a Regimental Board at Newbridge, Ireland (then the 11th's Depot). There his discharge was formally proposed, he being unfit for further military service from 'chronic rheumatism consequent on long service.

This last mention relates to the award to him in May 1854 of the Long Service and Good Conduct Medal, particulars of which are to be found at Kew, photographed from the original lists, as are those of the award of his Crimea Medal, with clasps for action at Alma, Balaclava, Inkerman and Sebastopol.

He was discharged on Tuesday, September 11, 1855. On the same day he was recorded in the Chelsea Hospital Registers (also at Kew) as an outpatient with a pension of 1s 8d per day. He was aged 46, and had served for more than 25 years.

From the Chelsea Registers and Returns of Changes among 'Out Pensioners' of Chelsea, it is seen that Charles drew his pension at first from Dublin, where it is obvious Elizabeth had remained while he was in the Crimea. From November 1, 1857, just over two years after his discharge, however, payment was transferred to the North London District.

Later on, a note in the Chelsea Hospital Registers of the date of Charles' death, on being checked at St Catherine's House, showed that his death had been registered at St George's, Hanover Square, Registration District. The 1861 Census for that part of London shows Charles, a farrier, at 28 Shepherd Street, Mayfair, with Elizabeth, and their son Charles Thomas.'

Charles Avison died at 28 Shepherd Street on May 14, 1865, at the age of 56.

How many more similar life stories must there be waiting to be discovered? Farrier Major Avison was not from a wealthy or a well-known family, he was not blessed with any outstanding characteristics, he was just an ordinary person, who, through fate, happened to live in, and be part of, one of the best-known periods of our history, the Crimean war. He no doubt saw Florence Nightingale, and he possibly was an escort to Queen Victoria's husband-to-be. If he didn't actually take part in the 'Charge of the Light Brigade' he was certainly on the spot soon afterwards. Richard's story gives us an insight to the life and mostly hard times of our ancestors.

Don't rush things

It is so easy to browse through books such as this one, and on the spur of the moment decide to attempt to trace your family tree. It is also very easy to set about it in a haphazard fashion and cause yourself many problems and a great deal of unnecessary expense.

If, for instance, your name is Turpin, and family stories tell you that you are connected with the famous highwayman, never let this idea obsess you throughout your research; just treat it as an interesting possibility. You must start with yourself, work back through your parents to your grandparents and from there on, take each generation as it comes. Above all, you must be methodical. Devise a simple system of collecting and storing your information at the beginning, as more complicated files for cross-referencing can be developed as time goes on. The Federation of Family History Societies publishes a number of easy-to-use recording files. Many people use a computer, but this is really best left until you have gained some experience with the basic methods.

One of the most important things to do is to read as many books for beginners as possible. Scattered throughout this handbook you will find highly recommended publications, either of a general nature or specializing in certain aspects of the subject. Some of these can be borrowed through your library service, or purchased from bookshops or from the publisher. *Family Tree Magazine* lists books for sale by post.

After reading this book, and before jumping in at the 'deep end', just spend some time deep in thought. We will show you the sensible way to approach the subject to enable you to save time and money.

We will inform you of a large number of possible basic sources; there are many more, of course, but you will discover these mainly as spin-offs from current research. We will also show you how to compile your tree.

We wish you good luck and hope you spend many enjoyable hours in the years to come as you go back in time. You will be pleasantly surprised at the number of people interested in the subject, and in the way the hobby encourages friendship and companionship amongst its participants.

Jean Cole and Michael Armstrong

CHAPTER 1

Where and How to Start

There are many ways to record the results of your research, but initially it is wise to use the system below. It is simple, straightforward, and easy to read.

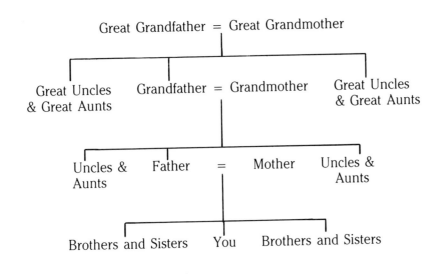

= means 'married to'

First, it is wise to make a basic family tree from the facts and information you already know. From this tree it is possible to see at a glance what family information you have. Many questions will remain to be asked from other members of the family who can fill in some of the gaps and supply documents and papers to give more names, dates, places and facts.

The Smith Family — an example

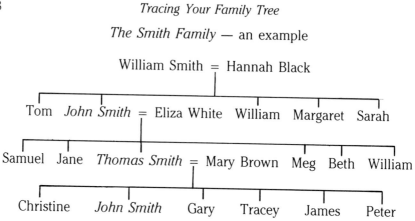

Start with the birth of the eldest child on the left hand side of the tree and so on along the line to the youngest at the right hand side of the chart. Fill in dates of births, deaths, marriages as far as you know on your basic tree.

Which family are you going to trace?

Which family line are you going to trace? Your father's, or paternal line? Your mother's, or maternal line? All families make fascinating research, taking different directions and social patterns in their lifetimes. One family may have been extremely affluent, another reasonably well-off and another may have been poor, existing on parish hand-outs or maybe eking out an existence in the workhouse; another family may have had more than its fair share of wrongdoers and eccentrics.

Some researchers decide to look into their paternal line only, but it is just as interesting to work on the maternal and female lines who married your direct ancestors as well. If you happen to be 'stuck' on one line for a while you are more likely to have success with another family whilst waiting to solve that particular problem. Maybe it is easier to trace one family about whom you know the most, or the one who lives nearest. Whichever you decide, always make a separate chart for each family line.

Family history research is a step-by-step process, starting with yourself, and, from the information given on your birth certificate, going back a generation to your parents and their marriage certificate. From the details given on this certificate you will then need to find your parents' birth certificates. From their births back to your grandparents' marriage, and back to their births, and so on, following this pattern. From you and your parents you will find you have four grandparents, eight great-grandparents, sixteen great-great-grandparents, doubling up every generation.

Obviously, as you progress back in time the blood line will become somewhat diluted, but all these family lines can make research an intriguing and gripping pursuit. It is a very true saying that 'truth can be stranger than fiction' and truth can be a great deal more interesting than fiction when it comes to one's very own family!

Ask the family

This is your first point of contact — your parents, grandparents, aunts, uncles, cousins, second cousins, and even close family friends. In this way you should be able to find relatives and cousins whom you previously had not known existed. You will find that one or two of these will be interested in the family history and who will be prepared to help with information. You will discover that every member of the family has a different piece which will fit into the family jig-saw puzzle.

Ask everyone for their memories and if they have any documents, letters, diaries, certificates and wills, etc. Visit them, talk and record everything you are told — do not rely on memory, it will only fail when you try to remember crucial names, dates and facts. Discreet tape-recording can be a great help at this time. Perhaps someone else from the family could go with you to write down the information in a notebook.

Some questions to ask:

- Is there a family bible giving dates of family events such as births, christenings, marriages, deaths and burials?

Phillips Family Bible

Baptismal Certificate dated 1906

- Are there any certificates of births, marriages and deaths?
- Has anyone kept baptismal certificates, confirmation cards, Sunday school prizes, burial or grave records, memorial cards?
- Has anyone in the family a diary, letters, birthday books?
- What about a family photograph album and other photographs? All of these need names, dates and places.

Exclusive Right of Burial Grant

- Has anyone been an apprentice? If so, are there any apprenticeship indentures?
- What are the occupations and trades in the family? Any trade union records?
- Where did members of the family go to school? Any school reports, school prizes or achievements?
- Has anyone served in the forces — army, navy, airforce, merchant navy? Any certificates of discharge, service, medals? Is there a tradition of service in the armed forces?
- Any other family papers? Passports, driving licence, ration books, identity cards?
- Has a particular name been handed down throughout the family?
- Did the family come from a certain town or county or did they come from elsewhere to settle in this country? Did anyone emigrate?
- Is the family Church of England or chapel or another religion?

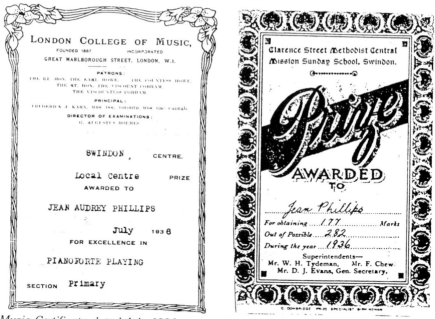

Music Certificate dated July 1936   Methodist Sunday School 1936

● Lastly, and very importantly, any remembered details of the earliest known members of the family?

Ask if anyone else in the family has done any work on tracing the family tree; if so, all research by someone else must be checked by you to ensure it is correct and perhaps amended and extended where necessary.

Recording information

At the very beginning of research it is vital to decide on a system for recording all the information gathered. It may be that a card index system, with a card for each ancestor and his family is the best for you, or a ring-file for each family in which can be inserted the results of research together with family documents, civil registration certificates and other records with plastic pocket files for photocopies and original documents.

It is absolutely essential that all transcribing from original documents be written exactly as it appears and *not* how you think it should be. Always record the date of research, where it was acquired, with the appropriate reference or catalogue numbers, even to recording negative or unproductive research so that the same ground need not be gone over again.

As more information is gathered together it can be added to your basic family tree. It won't be long before a larger sheet of paper is required. Always make sure everyone of the same generation is kept on a level line.

A family tree should always include names, dates of events, places and other

Canadian Marriage Certificate dated 1897

necessary information. A special research file with plenty of paper should be kept for visits to record offices and libraries, together with an ordnance survey map of the area you are going to search, preferably a one inch or half inch to the mile, a county parish map which shows every parish and will juris- dictions, plus a magnifying glass, a good supply of pencils, and a working family tree so that it is easy to see where the next path of research lies. Do your homework before setting out, and during your work keep a notebook handy to jot down any ideas or sources as they occur to you. If this is not done then valuable time will be wasted.

1915 Empire Day Certificate

Standard abbreviations should be used, such as:

B	Birth	soj	sojourner
Bur	Burial	lic.	by licence
s	son	Wp.	Will proved
sp	spinster	Inv.	Inventory
tp	this parish	C	Christened/baptized
ban	by banns	dau	daughter
C.O.G.	Consent of Guardians	wid	widow/widower
W	Will	wit	witness
Bd.	Bond	otp	of this parish
M or =	Marriage	C.O.P.	Consent of Parents
D	Death	Admon	Letters of
Unm	Unmarried		administration
bach	bachelor	M.I.	Monumental Inscription

Computers

There are now many genealogical software programs on the market. Some are very good, whilst others are limited in their capacity to store, sort and print out information in a suitable manner.

Before buying a package we would recommend caution.

Try to find someone who has had experience with a good one, and follow their advice.

Golden rules for research

Never assume: Check all family stories with facts.

Write everything down — do not rely on memory.
Methodically record all research.
Try to double check facts with legal documents.
Always do your homework.
And remember, your ultimate aim is to write your family history.

Further reading

Parish maps with will jurisdictions from the Institute of Heraldic and Genealogical Studies, Northgate, Canterbury, Kent.

The Phillimore Atlas and Index of Parish Registers ed. by C.R. Humphery-Smith, (Phillimore).

Computers for Family History by D. Hawgood, (Hawgood Computing 1985).

How to record Your Family Tree by Patrick Palgrave-Moore, (Elvery-Dowers, 1979).

A Genealogical and Historical Map of Ireland, (Heraldic Artists Dublin).

Note Taking and Keeping for Genealogists (Society of Genealogists Leaflet No. 4).

Interviewing Elderly Relatives Eve McLaughlin (FFHS).

Tracing Your Family History by Jean A. Cole (*Family Tree Magazine* 1988).

Series of National Genealogical Directories ed. by M. J. Burchall from 1979 and I. Caley from 1987.

Genealogical Research Directories ed. by Keith A. Johnson and Malcolm R. Sainty from 1982 onwards.

Register of One-Name Studies (5th ed. 1987) from the Guild of One-Name Studies, Box G.14 Charterhouse Buildings, Goswell Road, London, EC1M 7BA.

CHAPTER 2

Civil Registration of Births, Marriages and Deaths

The government decided that from 1 July 1837 all births, marriages and deaths taking place in England and Wales should be civilly recorded and certificates issued to each person concerned. Copies of the records were to be kept both locally at a register office and centrally in London. This did not mean the recording of the events in the religious houses would cease, it meant instead that people had the choice of a religious and a civil ceremony or just a civil one.

As far as marriages were concerned, the local community religious leader could be licensed to perform the appropriate ceremonies on behalf of the state as well as his own religion. If he was not licensed, a registrar would do the work involved. The other alternative was a visit to the Register Office solely for a civil wedding which had to be by notice of marriage or by licence. In theory, all births, marriages and deaths should be found duly recorded; in fact, some are not, particularly in the case of births.

Many people viewed the introduction of the system, as they did the census registration which followed in 1841, with a certain amount of suspicion. At the time when only the houses of religion looked after the christenings, some couples never bothered with a ceremony; others left it until they had a number of children, having them all christened together. Many never bothered at all, so in the early days of civil registration the same kind of attitude persisted and many births were never recorded. However, by 1875 penalties came into force for non-registration of births.

I heard of one case where a boy was born and baptized Edward and who promptly died. In the next eight years a series of children were born and all christened with various names. Ten years after the birth of Edward, the last boy of the family came along and he, too, was given the name Edward. Later in life, the second Edward had reason to need his birth certificate, but by this time both his parents had died and he had never even remembered seeing a copy of the certificate. The repository indexes were searched and he was most puzzled to find there was no mention of his name at the time when there should have been. He later mentioned this to an older member of the family who informed him that he had had an older brother named Edward who had died, and when his parents chose to call him Edward too, they decided that, as they had already had one Edward recorded and baptized there would be no need to go through the same procedure again and register the boy. After learning of this, Edward went back and promptly found the record of his elder brother and obtained a certificate, using it whenever a certificate was required for the rest of his life. Needless to say, he enjoyed a very long and happy retirement.

All the way along the road of ancestral research you must expect many pitfalls, caused mostly by human error, or even at times sheer dishonesty, but it is things like this which help to make the hobby so fascinating.

St. Catherine's House

You will no doubt have noticed that only England and Wales have been mentioned so far. Civil registration started later in other parts of Britain, more details of this are given later in this chapter. The central repository for all registered births, marriages and deaths in England and Wales is at the General Register Office, St. Catherine's House, 10 Kingsway, Aldwych, London WC2B 6JP. This is a large building situated on the corner of Kingsway and Aldwych. Two tube stations are within easy walking distance, one is Holborn on the Piccadilly line at the top end of Kingsway, and the other is Temple on the District and Circle lines on the Embankment. Numerous buses pass the door of St. Catherine's House, coming from various directions. The opening hours are 08.30—16.30 Monday to Friday, always closing at the weekends and Bank holidays.

One is allowed to conduct a personal search of the indexes free of charge. You are, however, not able to see the actual original copy of the certificates. To obtain one of these, the reference to the event must be found in the indexes and an application form filled in. The completed form is then taken to the cashier's desk and a statutory fee paid. Your copy of the certificate will then be sent through the post and you can normally expect a wait of up to 21 days for this to arrive at your home.

If, however, you are able to call back two days later you may collect your certificates, but this must be arranged at the same time that you pay for them. The fee is revised from time to time (needless to say, usually upward!). Charges may be obtained by applying to St. Catherine's House by post or telephone. There are a number of staff in the building to answer queries from researchers, but the same thing happens there as it does when you want a policeman — you can seldom find one. In this case, never be afraid to ask a fellow researcher if you have a problem, most are more than willing to pass on their knowledge. Try to avoid the ones who look like solicitors or their clerks — they usually have little time for family historians.

The staff of St. Catherine's will conduct a small amount of research for postal applicants for up to a five year period. To qualify for this you must send the fee, which is usually twice that of a personal application. If the searcher is unable to locate your particular entry, around 60 per cent of the fee is refunded.

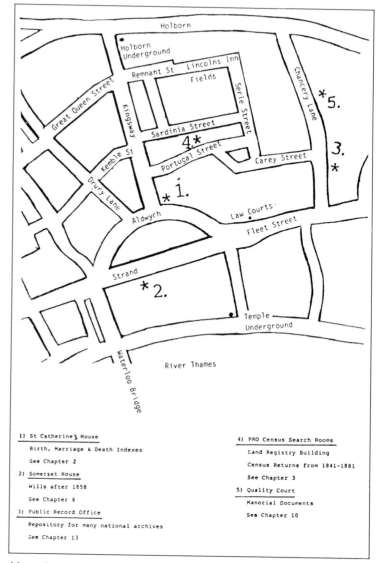

Map of part of London, showing some of the more important record repositories

There are also a number of professional genealogists and Family History Societies, who provide certificate finding services for about the same price. Some of these often advertise in *Family Tree Magazine,* the Society of Genealogists' publication *The Genealogists' Magazine,* or even in some of the local Family History Society journals.

Go prepared

Before even attempting to delve into either civil or any other repository held

St. Catherine's House, London.

records it is wise to follow the well-trodden path of preliminary research at family source. It is so easy to pay good money for a certificate only to find that Great Aunt Maude had a copy of the same one hidden away in a 'safe place'. It is surprising what sources can be tackled before a visit to St. Catherine's, and these are dealt with in Chapter 1.

St. Catherine's itself is a very large place but it does get crowded. Body heat generated by a number of highly active people ensures that the inside of the building gets very warm at times, so don't go dressed in heavy warm clothes which cannot be removed. People who are fighting against time generate more heat than usual. Try also, to avoid going loaded down with large bags or other luggage. It is best not to take young children unless they are old enough to do some useful research themselves as they tend to get bored and cause a great deal of annoyance to other people. Don't take the dog either! As in other similar places the consumption of food or drink is not permitted in the search room; in fact there are no eating or drinking facilities at all in St. Catherine's, but there are decent toilets and washbasins, and a number of eating houses may be found within a reasonable distance of the building.

Many a conversation between family historians eventually introduces the subject of, 'I remember the first time I went to St. Catherine's . . .' This is then followed by some amusing story, such as when a fat person got wedged between the wall and the end of the bookshelf, or when a lady was arguing with the man whom she said put his book down on her space whilst she was getting another volume from the shelves.

It is doubtful if there is another place in Britain quite like St. Catherine's. Those who have never visited it have missed an experience of a lifetime. It is the kind of place where magistrates should send criminal offenders for seven days instead of a twenty-five year sentence of hard labour! I am, of course, exaggerating, but even if you never really have to go to St. Catherine's it is well worth a visit anyway just to see how it operates.

The system

In all three departments, the record volumes of births, marriages and deaths are in quarters, ending March, June, September and December each year. Always remember that 42 days were allowed in which to register a birth, so if the entry is not in the quarter you think it should be in, try the following one.

Each quarter is arranged in alphabetical order. The early volumes were written in free hand so there are usually more volumes in these sections. As type was introduced, more details were condensed into each book, so consequently the number of entries in each volume is higher. When you are unsure of the exact date for the year in which you are searching, it is sensible to resort to a methodical approach. You have to bear in mind the fact that there are often other people looking for dates around the same time as yourself, so if you have looked first in March followed by June you may then find that the September one is missing. Instead of waiting for its return it makes sense to go on to December and then back to September when it is back in its place. This will save a lot of time in the long run. A very simple aid can be devised, all you need is a piece of notepaper and a pen or pencil, and draw something like this.

Year	M	J	S	D
1880				
1881				
1882				
1883				
1884				

It is a simple task then to tick off the period you have searched. After a while it is so easy to forget which book you have already looked at, so such a system is a 'must'.

When you open an early birth index volume you will see it set out in this fashion:-

Surname	Forename(s)	Supt. Reg. District	Vol.	Page
JOHNSON	John R.	Basford	7b	251
JOHNSON	John S.	Birmingham	6d	314
JOHNSON	John T.	Huntingdon	3b	196

From September 1911 the maiden name of the mother is included in the indexes, so the above list would then look like this:-

Surname	Forename(s)	Maiden name of Mother	Supt.Reg. District	Vol.	Page
JOHNSON	John R.	MORGAN	Basford	7b	251
JOHNSON	John S.	SMITHURST	Birmingham	6d	314
JOHNSON	John T.	NEIL	Huntingdon	3b	196

As you can see, this is much easier later than the earlier layouts.

There might, however, be twenty John Johnsons, some with a second Christian name, which is always seen as an initial in the indexes, and some without a second name. This is where you have to be very careful when you do your homework, as you may think that your particular John did not have a middle name and that he was born in the Basford area of Nottingham. There is no point in applying for a certificate in the name of John R. just because he is from the Basford registration area. Only when you are perfectly sure that there seem to be no Johns without a middle name, should you again focus your attention on the John R. Then you should begin to wonder just how well you did your homework in the first place. Unless you want to take the risk of wasting your money by applying for a wrong certificate, first try to find out from other sources if John did have a second Christian name. A slap-happy approach can make the hobby expensive and very frustrating.

Searching for a marriage certificate will follow a similar pattern. When using the very early indexes, if you are looking, for instance, for the marriage of Herbert Bowskill and Jean Summers, you will first have to look in the 'B's' for Bowskill, Herbert, and then in the letter 'S' for Summers, Jean. Before March 1912, apart from the reference numbers and the same year quarter, there is no indication that these two people were married to each other. So, if the wedding took place in the Basford area you would first of all find:- BOWSKILL, Herbert. Basford 7b 124 in the June quarter of 1900 and then:- SUMMERS, Jean. Basford 7b 124 in the June quarter of 1900. It is important that all the reference numbers and the year and quarter tally, for if they do not then you will waste your money if you order a certificate, as it will not be the right one.

After March 1912 things get a little easier, for in the lists we see:-

Surname	Forename(s)	Surname of Spouse	Supt. Reg. District	Vol.	Page
BOWSKILL	Herbert	SUMMERS	Basford	7b	124
(continue in the 'S' lists)					
SUMMERS	Jean	BOWSKILL	Basford	7b	124

Again, the same method of approach is used in searching for death certificates. When we open the pages of the early volumes we just see:-

Surname	Forename(s)		Supt. Reg. District	Vol.	Page
THOMAS	Herbert R.		Basford	7b	191

(From June 1866 the age at death is added as given by the informant.)

Surname	Forename(s)	Age	Supt.Reg. District	Vol.	Page
THOMAS	Herbert R.	61	Basford	7b	191

After 1969 the date of birth, if known, is also shown, but this should be checked with other sources when you get the chance. When searching the indexes containing the age at death, it is worth bearing in mind that the informant could have been anyone from a spouse to a person who only knew the deceased socially, and who had a guess at the age, so be very careful not to take this for granted and always check from other sources.

When you first walk into St. Catherine's House it is easy to spot which department the birth indexes are in, because the books are red. All the marriages are bound in green covers, and the deaths in black.

Let us now consider how and what information can be gleaned from the various civil certificates. As with all family history research, one should begin from the present and work back in time. Starting with your own birth certificate you will know that your name could be Robert John Holloway and that you were born on 19 January 1954 at 12 Newton Street, Derby. Your father at the time of registration was a plumber's mate by the name of George Holloway and your mother's name was Mary and her maiden name was Ellison. Also included will be the date of registration and the name and address of the informant. It is easy to learn at this stage if the informant could write or not, for, if not, there would be a cross at the side of the name. If your mother had been married before her previous married name should also be included, along with her maiden name.

The birth certificate of an illegitimate child very often has a blank space

Civil Registration (Birth)

Civil Registration (Marriage)

where the father's name should be (see index for references to Illegitimacy in other chapters). Otherwise, from your birth certificate you should now know the name of your father and mother's maiden name. This information should, in most cases, enable you to search for their marriage certificate.

From a marriage certificate you should learn the date of marriage; name of the house of worship or register office, by banns, notice or licence, the name of your father, his age at marriage (over 21 years is often shown as 'full age'), whether he was a bachelor, widower or divorcee, his occupation and where he lived at the time of the event; also included is his father's name and occupation and whether deceased. The same information is given in the case of the bride. Also learned is whether the couple could write, the name of the officiating officer or priest, and, a very important point to note, the names of the witnesses. These can be relatives or friends. The information gained from this certificate will enable you then to have learned enough to obtain the birth certificates of your parents, after which you will require the marriage certificates of their parents.

Civil Registration (Death)

Less information is gained from death certificates than from the birth or marriage ones, but nevertheless, as many sources should be used as possible in tracing a family history. The death certificates tells us the name, sex and address of the deceased, the age, as given by the informant, and the place of death. Also included is the occupation of men and single women, or the name and occupation of a husband for a married woman, or a father for a child. Also there is the cause of death, the date of registration and the name of the informant, the registrar's name and the district and sub-district.

Other Records at St. Catherine's House

There are other records available besides the birth, marriage and death indexes at St. Catherine's House, and these are:-

The Miscellaneous Returns

- The Army Chaplain's Registers: Births from 1760 to 1955; Marriages from 1796 to 1955 and Deaths from 1761 to 1970.
- Consular births, marriages and deaths from 1849 to 1965.
- Deaths abroad 1951 to 1970s.
- Births and Deaths in aircraft (registered in Gt. Britain) from 1949.
- Deaths at Sea (Marine Deaths) 1837 to 1965.
- Marriages on H.M. Ships 1849 to 1889.
- Marriages abroad, miscellaneous 1946 to 1970.
- Commonwealth Marriages 1947 to 1965.
- U.K. High Commission Deaths 1950 to 1965.
- Royal Air Force Returns from 1920.
- War Deaths:-Army Officers 1914 to 1921, 1939 to 1945.
             Army Other Ranks 1914 to 1921, 1939 to 1945.
             Naval Officers 1914 to 1921, 1939 to 1945.
             Navy (other ranks) 1914 to 1921, 1939 to 1945.
             RAF 1939 to 1945.
             South Africa 1899 to 1902.
- Adoptions from 1927 — only short form certificates with adoptive parents' names, date of birth and adoption will be issued to the public. Full adoption certificates are only issued to the adopted person and are obtainable from The General Register Office, Registration Division, Titchfield, Fareham, Hants PO15 5RU.
- From 1927, there is a register of stillbirths but this must be requested at the enquiry office at St. Catherine's House.
- Foundlings are to be found after 'Z' at the end of the birth indexes for each quarter.
- Shipping and Seamen's Records are at the Registrar General, Llandaff, Cardiff, from 1890. The indexes will be searched on receipt of the appropriate fee (records previous to 1890 have been deposited at the Public Record Office, Kew, Surrey under the records of the British Transport [BT].

Scotland

The Scottish civil registration system started on 1 January 1855 and the records for the whole of Scotland are kept at New Register House, Edinburgh. I must mention in passing that this building also houses the old parish records as there are no county record offices like there are in England and Wales.

Needless to say, record searching in Scotland is usually much easier than in England. The Scottish authorities also charge fees for certificates ordered through the post. A 'plus' is that you can actually see the copies of the certificates whilst you are on the premises.

Another difference between Scotland and St. Catherine's is that you must pay to enter the building. Copying notes of certificates is then free, but you must, of course, pay if you require to take official copies home, but even then they are cheaper than those in England.

You may obtain details of the search facilities and charges by sending a stamped addressed envelope to the General Register Office for Scotland, New Register House, Edinburgh EH1 3YT.

Scottish records are reckoned to be more informative than those in England, and, from my own experience, I am bound to agree. Birth certificates give the name and surname of the child; place and date of birth, sex, name and maiden name of mother, and, after 1861, the date of marriage; signature and qualifications of informant; place of residence, if different from place of birth; date and place of registration, and signature of registrar.

The marriage certificate informs when and how married, eg. by banns or licence; full names; signature; rank or occupation and state of parties, with ages; residence; names; rank or occupation of fathers of both the bride and groom, and the names and surnames of the mothers.

Death certificates include name; surname; rank or occupation; marital status of deceased; when and where died; sex and age; name; surname; rank or occupation of father; name and maiden name of mother; cause of death; name of certifying physician; signature and qualifications of informant, and place of residence.

Often the letters RCE appear in the margin with a reference number — this means 'Register of Corrected Entries' and usually refers to the fact there has been a change of name.

In Scotland you can fill your complete day, for when you have dealt with civil records you are then able to go on to the parish records without leaving the building. Many of the later civil records are now kept on microfiche.

Other Scottish sources of information

Registers of stillbirths from 1939 — these are records compiled by district registrars but are not open to public scrutiny. Extracts will only be issued in exceptional circumstances (e.g. legal purposes).

Adopted Children Register from 1930 — these are records of persons adopted under orders made by the Scottish Courts. There are no entries relating to persons born before October 1909.

Births, deaths and marriages outside Scotland

Marine Register of births and deaths from 1855. Certified returns received from the Registrar General for Shipping and Seamen in respect of births and deaths on British registered merchant vessels at sea if the child's father or the deceased person was a Scottish subject.

Air Registers of births and deaths from 1948. Records of births and deaths in any part of the world in aircraft registered in the United Kingdom where it appears that the child's father or the deceased person was usually resident in Scotland.

Service Records from 1881. These include Army returns of births, deaths and marriages of Scottish persons at military stations abroad during the period 1881 to 1959, and the Service Department Registers which since 1 April 1959 have recorded births, marriages and deaths outside the UK relating to persons ordinarily resident in Scotland who are serving in or are employed by H.M. Forces. It includes the families of members of the forces, also certified copies of entries relating to marriages solemnized outside the UK by army chaplains since 1892 where one of the parties to the marriage is described as Scottish and at least one of the parties is serving in H.M. Forces.

War Registers from 1899. There are three registers: South African War (1899–1902) which records the deaths of Scottish soldiers; World War I (1914 to 1919) which records the deaths of Scottish persons serving as Warrant officers, non-commissioned officers or men in the army or as Petty officers or men in the Royal Navy; World War II (1939 to 1945) which consists of incomplete returns of the deaths of Scottish members of the armed forces.

Consular Returns of births, marriages and deaths from 1914. Certified copies of registrations by British Consuls relating to persons of Scottish birth or descent. Records of births and deaths date from 1914 and marriages from 1917.

High Commissions Returns of births and deaths from 1964. These are returns from certain Commonwealth countries relating to persons of Scottish descent or birth. Some earlier returns are available for India, Pakistan, Bangladesh, Sri Lanka, and Ghana, and some returns are available for marriages in certain other countries.

Registers of births, deaths and marriages in foreign countries from 1850 to 1965. Records compiled by the General Register Office until the end of 1965 relating to the births of children of Scottish parents, and the marriages and deaths of Scottish subjects. The entries were made on the basis of information supplied by the parties concerned and after consideration of the evidence of each event.

Foreign Marriages from 1947. Certified copies of certificates (with translations) relating to marriages of persons from Scotland in certain foreign countrie⌐

according to the laws of those countries without the presence of the British Consular Officer.

From 1 May 1984 a central register of divorces in Scotland is maintained. Extracts from the register show the names of the parties; the date and place of marriage; the date and place and details of any order made by the court regarding financial provision or custody of children. From this date also GRO staff ceased to mark marriage entries to indicate a divorce had occurred.

Ireland

Yet another starting date to remember is that for Ireland. General registration started there in 1864. Irish genealogy is a positive minefield. In 1922 the Four Courts of Dublin was badly damaged during unrest, and many of the Irish records destroyed.

Available records from 1864 to 1922, including non Roman Catholic marriages from 1 April, 1845, are held at the Office of the Registrar General, Joyce House, 8–11 Lombard Street, Dublin 2. From 1922 onwards, all records of Southern Ireland are held there, and those of the North are held by the General Register Office, Oxford House, 49–55 Chichester Street, Belfast BT1 4HL. Details of the records available, and charges, may be obtained from both the offices named.

It would be worthwhile to read as many specialist books on Irish research as possible before contemplating tackling this aspect of civil research.

Birth, marriage and death certificates, and indexes in the possession of the local District Superintendent Registrar

If you have visited St. Catherine's House and been unable to discover a birth, marriage or death for someone, then it maybe that, in some way or another, it has 'slipped through the net' between the local registrar's returns and the Registrar General.

If you happen to know the district where the event took place it could be a good idea to contact the district registrar and ask for a search of the indexes, but you must know an approximate date to within a couple of years or so, and also supply names and places as far as you know, for they will only do a five year search. The Superintendent Registrar's indexes and certificates relate only to events which took place in his district.

It can be of tremendous help when you know an area, particularly if the surname you are seeking is quite a common one, for the indexes at St. Catherine's House may have literally hundreds of entries for that name from all over England and Wales. The local registrar's indexes may narrow the odds somewhat in this respect.

If you decide you would like to make a personal search of the district registrar's indexes, then for a fee of a few pounds you may do so for up to six hours which may be split into two or three visits. For this fee the registrar or his staff will check to see if the references you have chosen are the ones you require; this he will do up to a certain number of entries. If you decide from these references that you would like a certificate the usual fee will apply, just as it does in St. Catherine's House on a personal search. If you need one specific certificate and you have the relevant details you may apply direct through the post to the district registrar.

If you feel you would like to make a personal check, do telephone or write to the Superintendent Registrar of the office concerned first to make an appointment. Addresses will be found in a telephone directory of the area, or your own local Superintendent Registrar of births, marriages and deaths will be able to supply an address for you.

Some church marriage registers from 1837 may have been deposited in local county record offices and if this is so, this is another source for you to seek the marriage you require where you can make a copy of the entry without paying the normal registrar's required fee. Many county record offices do not allow photocopying of their registers anymore, but will be more than happy to give you a form stating that the entry you have found is a true entry from the marriage register.

Comments

- If the time of birth has been given on a birth certificate after 1839 it may mean the birth was of a twin or a multiple birth. Up to 1839 the time of birth could be given for a single birth.
- A child may not always be given the same forenames on a birth certificate and a baptismal certificate. Parents may have changed their minds between registration and baptism.
- Marriage in a register office will either be by notice or licence.
- Do not be adamant about occupations, as our forebears were likely to change occupations or give different ones on various registration certificates.
- There were two copies of a marriage certificate, besides the one given to the bride and groom, one for the church and a copy for the registrar. The church register may be deposited in a county record office or may still be with the incumbent of the parish.
- Death indexes after 1866 give the ages of deceased — if just '0' is given, it means an infant death.
- Always look at the end of the surname spelling in the indexes, as children who have not been named will be shown at the end of each surname spelling under male or female.
- A marriage could take place in a register office from 1 July 1837.
- If unable to find a marriage, make a wider search using birth indexes to find children of the marriage. The marriage may have taken place years before the birth of the first child or some years after the birth of the first child.
- Ages — our ancestors frequently lied about their ages, and on marriage certificates ages have often been falsified. It was a crime punishable by law, but as long as a couple stated they were over 21 years and the registrar

or minister was satisfied, the marriage could go ahead. The 1836 Marriage Act made no provision for the production of a birth certificate or baptismal certificate.

● Column five of a birth certificate gives name, surname, and maiden name of mother. When looking for a marriage using the maiden name of a mother as shown on a birth certificate, and you are unable to find a marriage, it may be that the mother has been married before and widowed, and her widowed name has not been given on the birth certificate. Try a census return of the same period or other methods to find more family information.

● In years gone by it was a very common practice to give a child the same name as an older brother or sister who had died. So if you find two children with the same Christian name, the chances are you will find a burial entry concerning the first one.

● The information given at the time of registration of a birth, marriage or death is considered to be the true facts by law, and this will remain despite any amendments or alterations made afterwards by the registrar. Therefore indexes will only show details of the certificate as given at the time of registration of the event and not any subsequent amendments. When you have reached the stage where your earliest currently known ancestor can be found in the census returns, it is much more economical to turn in that direction.

Further reading

St Catherine's House by Eve McLaughlin (McLaughlin Guides).

How to Trace Your Family History in Northern Ireland by Kathleen Neill (Irish Heritage Association 1986).

Handbook on Irish Genealogy (How to trace your ancestors and relatives in Ireland) (Heraldic Artists, Dublin 1980).

Scottish Roots (a step-by-step guide for ancestor hunters in Scotland and overseas) by Alwyn James (MacDonald 1981).

In Search of Scottish Ancestry by G. Hamilton Edwards (Phillimore 1972).

The Ancestor Trail in Ireland by D. F. Begley (Heraldic Artists 1987).

Irish Genealogy (a record finder) by D. F. Begley (Heraldic Artists 1987).

A Genealogical and Historical Map of Ireland (Heraldic Artists).

CHAPTER 3

The Census Returns and Some Tax Records

Censuses of population have been taken from ancient times, such as the one recorded in the Bible at the time of the birth of Jesus Christ. Later on, a most important census, Domesday, was carried out in 1086 in England. As the population grew, it was deemed necessary to start taking a census. The first officially recorded one was in Sweden in 1749. Although a bill was introduced into Parliament in England for a census of the population in 1753, it failed because of the government's opposition to the whole idea. It was not until 10 March 1801, some forty years after Scotland had carried out its own, that the first official census of England and Wales, the Channel Islands, and the Isle of Man was taken.

The results revealed that the total population of England and Wales in that year was just under 9 million, and by the 1851 census it had increased to nearly 18 million souls. This was mainly due to better living conditions and larger families.

The Population of England and Wales in millions of persons at the time of the first census

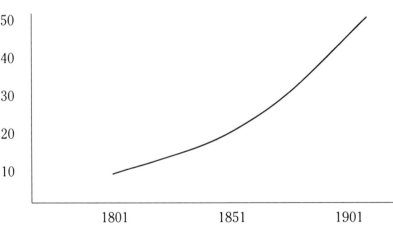

Over this period many people left the country to live in towns and cities because there was more work in mills and factories. In 1801, 75 per cent of the population lived in the country, but by 1851, 54 per cent lived and worked in urban areas. By the 1901 census it was discovered that only 30 per cent of the population still lived in the countryside. The population of Scotland and Ireland also increased throughout these years, but not so dramatically as in England and Wales.

The year 1801 was the time of the Napoleonic Wars, with the ever constant threat of invasion, and men were needed for the army and navy for the defence of the country against the enemy. There were now more poor than ever claiming relief from their parishes, and it was from around this time that the State showed signs of taking control of the country. It was at this period that the first Income Tax was imposed, and ordnance surveys of the country commenced, as well as the population census. The census has been taken every ten years from 1801 to the present day, except for 1941 during the height of the second world war. The returns for 1931 were destroyed by enemy action during a bombing raid in World War II.

The 1801 census was put into the hands of the parish elders who duly carried out the counting of persons within their parish. These returns gave the number of people in a parish, together with inhabited and uninhabited houses, and classified occupations within a broad scope. When completed, the returns were sent to the government for analysis. This first census, therefore, and the following three 10-yearly ones are of no real use to the family historian, except for parish statistics, and it was not until 1841 that more questions were asked of the population in general.

Census forms were distributed by enumerators to each household in their designated area, just as happens today. The forms were collected, checked, and then entered into a printed book of blank forms provided for the purpose. For those of the population unable to read or write, and they were numerous, the enumerator or some other responsible person, such as the parish clerk or the schoolmaster, would fill in the census forms for them and assist others who were unsure as to exactly just what was required of them.

All census returns come under the 100 Year Old Rule and the ones which are currently available to the public are:

1841	7 June
1851	30 March
1861	7 April (Easter)
1871	2 April
1881	3 April

They were for all persons residing in a house or institution at midnight on these dates. So the 1841 census on 7 June was at midnight on 6/7 June, the 1851 for midnight on 30/31 March, and so on.

The 1841 census, although not so informative as subsequent censuses, is nevertheless, still of great value to the family historian.

Details required were:

1841 Census. 7 June, at midnight

1. Place (street name, house number or house name)
2. Houses — where inhabited, uninhabited or a building.
3. Names of each person who abode therein the preceding night, with surname and forename.
4. The columns for age and sex. Ages up to 15 years are correct. Over 15 years the ages were reduced to the nearest 5 years.
   For example: 53 years would show on the census return as rounded down to 50 years and 39 years would show as rounded down to 35 years.
5. Profession, Trade, Employment or of Independent Means.
6. Where born. Column to be marked Y for Yes, if born in the same county of residence, or N for No if born outside the county. The next column for:- If born in Scotland — S: Ireland — I: Foreign parts — F.
7. End of household.
8. End of building.

In this particular census, relationships to the head of the household are not given.

The 1851, 1861, 1871 and 1881 census give much more information.

1851 Census. 30 March, at midnight

1. Number of schedule filled in by the householder.
2. Name of street, place, or road with name or number of the house.
3. Name and surname of each person who resided in the house at midnight on the 30 March.
4. Relation to the Head of the family — including servants, lodgers, etc.
5. Condition — whether married, unmarried, widow or widower.
6. Age and sex. Actual age at the time of the census.
7. Rank, Profession or Occupation.
8. Where born. Place of birth.
9. Whether blind, deaf or dumb.

By 1871 and 1881, additional questions were asked in the column, 'whether blind, deaf and dumb', which was sub-divided into Deaf and Dumb: Blind: Imbecile or Idiot: Lunatic. Also in the 1881 census the question was asked — 'age last birthday?'. All relationships given from 1851 onwards were to the Head of the Household alone and *not* to each other.

PLACE	HOUSES Uninhabited or Building	HOUSES Inhabited	NAMES of each person who abode therein the preceding Night	AGE and SEX Male	AGE and SEX Female	PROFESSION, TRADE, EMPLOYMENT or of INDEPENDENT MEANS	Whether Born in Same County	Whether Born in Scotland, Ireland or Foreign Parts
Sheep Street [Marston Hill Wiltshire] Jn			Mary Sweetapple		45	Laundress	N	
			George Do	14		Appr.	Y	
			Flora McDonald		45	Annuitant		S
			John Herbert	20		Ag Lab	Y	
			Martha Do		25	Charwoman	Y	
			Elizabeth Do		7		N	
			Pierre Le Blanc	60		Independent		F
			Maria Do		55	Lacemaker		
			William Barrett	35		Miller and Baker	N	
			Lucy Do		20	Dressmaker	Y	
Jn			John Do	9			Y	
			Amelia Do		7		N	
			Jane Do		3		Y	
Jn			Mary O'Shea		65	F.S.		I
			Patrick O'Shea	65		M.S.		I
			Fred Moss	40		P clerk	Y	
			Purnell Do		40	Pauper Cripple	Y	
			Jo: Do	25		Weaver	Y	
			Winefride Do		20	Cloth worker	N.K	
			Katharine Do		2		N	

Fictitious example of an 1841 census

Where to find the census

The only place in England and Wales where the complete census returns for both countries plus the Channel Islands and the Isle of Man can be found is:-
The Census Search Rooms of the Public Record Office,
Land Registry Building,
Portugal Street,
London, WC2A 3HP.

Opening hours — Monday to Friday, 9.30 a.m. to 4.50 p.m. The rooms are not open on public holidays or the first two weeks in October.

The 1841 and 1851 censuses may also be consulted in the Rolls Room of the

1881 Census (RG 11) for the hamlet of Way in Cruwys Morchard, Devon

PRO Chancery Lane, by those with readers tickets. The returns for 1841 and
1851 form part of the class 'Census Returns' — HO (Home Office) 107.

The 1861 and the following census are in the class RG (Registrar General):

1861	RG 9
1871	RG 10
1881	RG 11

*1901 Census of Population for Wiltshire — a page from the book of
statistics*

The returns are arranged by enumeration districts, and it is reasonably easy to look at a parish or hamlet or even a small town, taking all families with the same surnames as the ones you are seeking. It is vital to look at neighbouring parishes for members of the family who may be working away from home or in service, as well as such institutions as the workhouse, prison, hospital, barracks, asylums, ships and, perhaps, the prison hulks which had prisoners confined awaiting transportation to the colonies.

Large towns and cities were divided amongst a number of districts and it is necessary to have some idea of an address of an ancestor before searching these, although it has been known for some desperate researchers to search methodically through a large town from beginning to end in an endeavour to find an ancestor when the address has not been known!

Indexes to the enumeration districts of parishes and towns are available in the Census room and there are street indexes for London and other cities and large towns.

The original census books are still in existence at the Public Record Office, Chancery Lane, London, but they have been microfilmed and it is *only* on these films that the searcher is able to read the census. A reader's ticket is not required for access to the Census Search rooms, although one is needed for anyone who wishes to consult other Public Record Office records in Chancery Lane or at Kew, when an application for a reader's ticket must be made in person (see Chapter 13).

When visiting the search rooms at Portugal Street it is wise to be there reasonably early to ensure a seat. After signing in, first find a seat and leave a coat, not a handbag, to show it is yours. If all the seats have been taken there will be a queue so join it straight away.

The Public Record Office issues a free leaflet on how to find and use the census, so do take one of these and study it carefully on your first visit; you can then familiarize yourself with the procedure on how to find the film reference you require.

Photocopies are available, and these are well worth the money so that you can add a copy of the census to your own family documentation.

A rest room is available for researchers at Portugal Street. Drinks may be obtained from a vending machine. People are allowed to consume their own food in that area, but not in the search rooms. Within the forseeable future, the Census Room in Portugal Street will be replaced by a reading room specifically designed for consulting microfilm.

Scottish census

Census returns were taken every ten years in Scotland just as in England and Wales, but there is an added bonus in that their 1891 Census is available to the public. They can be viewed at:

The General Register Office,
New Register House,
Edinburgh, EH1 2YT.

The Four Courts Dublin 1922. This picture was taken at the time of the riots when many Irish genealogical records were destroyed.

Irish census

Unfortunately, the returns for Ireland from 1821 to 1891 were destroyed, and therefore prior to 1901 returns are not generally available, although a few have survived for isolated areas. The 1901 and 1911 census returns are available to the public.

Contact: The Public Record Office of Ireland, Four Courts, Dublin, Ireland.

The Public Record Office of Northern Ireland, 66 Balmoral Avenue, Belfast, BT9 6NY, Northern Ireland.

Census returns of 1891 and 1901
The census returns of 1891 and 1901 for England, Wales, Channel Islands, and the Isle of Man are, at present, in the custody of the Registrar General, The Office of Population Censuses and Surveys, St. Catherine's House, London, and are closed to the public for 100 years. However, the Registrar General will supply a form for the use of a direct descendant or next of kin to apply to see one of these census returns. An exact address must be supplied, and the names required from the census; in return the enquirer will receive the surname, forename, age and place of birth of the persons named.

The fee for this service is very expensive but it may be worth the money to use this service on occasion when all other leads have dried up.

Applications should be made to:-
The Registrar General,
The Office of Population Censuses and Surveys,
St. Catherine's House,
Kingsway,
London, WC2B 6JP.

Census returns held elsewhere
There are copies of census microfilm in various local reference libraries and record offices but most of these refer only to their own particular locality or county.

Some individuals, and family history and local history societies are in the process of transcribing and indexing census for their area or county, and these can obviously be a short cut to finding out an address or area for your family.

There are booklets giving information as to where the census returns and indexes may be located, and these are of immense help in finding copies and indexes for your area.

Try writing to the secretary of the local family history society to find out if the particular census you are interested in has been indexed. His or her name may be obtained from the Headquarters of the Federation of Family History Societies. (The address can be found on page 170).

Tax and other records
Fortunately for the genealogist there are some records which act as a type of census. The following lists and tax records are such.

Some tax lists, together with other records such as muster rolls, militia lists, and subsidy rolls, operate on their own account by listing and naming population, and it is this type of documentation which helps the family historian trace a family back in time.

Occasionally, a parish or small town may have taken a census of its population for their own purposes and these are often found in with parish records (see Chapter 7).

Some abbreviations found in census returns

Ag. lab	Agricultural labourer
Ann.	Annuitant
App.	Apprentice
Bro.	Brother
Dau.	Daughter
Daughter in law	In addition to the present day definition (son's wife) it could also indicate a step-daughter
Dom.	Domestic servant
Emp.	Employed
F.S.	Female servant
H.	Head (of the household)
Illeg.	Illegitimate
Ind.	Independent (of Independent means)
Inf.	Infant
Lab.	Labourer
M.	Married
M.S.	Male servant
N.K.	Not known
Sis.	Sister
Soj.	Sojourner
Son in law	Also means step-son — see 'daughter in law'
U/Unm.	Unmarried
W.	Wife
Wid.	Widow/Widower
Vis.	Visitor

Some of the following records have been printed for some counties but, in the main, they are still in their original forms in record offices. They are numerous and varied in their content. Here is a selection:

Lay Subsidy Rolls from about 1332 onwards with lists of inhabitants of parishes and taxes due. They exist in some cases until the late seventeenth century (Public Record Office).

Recusant Rolls from 1592. These were annual returns of fines imposed on those who did not attend the established Church of England (Public Record Office and some county record offices).

Protestation Oath Returns 1641/2 for the entire country. These were returns of all males over 18 years of age who were in favour of the true Protestant religion. Those not in favour were also named. They were recorded for each parish within a county. (The House of Lords Record Office). In this same period of 1641/2, monies were raised by an Act of Parliament from every parish in the country for distressed Protestants in Ireland. This was for the relief of Protestant English immigrants in Ireland who were victims of the Catholic Irish at this time. (Public Record Office).

Association Oath Rolls 1696. The Act of Association in 1696 required anyone who held public office to take a solemn oath of Association for the better preservation of His Majesty's royal person and government. (Public Record Office and county record offices).

Hearth Taxes 1662-1689. These provide one of the most valuable sources for the country. Parishes in each county made a return of names and taxable hearths, including those poor people who were exempt from the tax. It was not a popular tax and many people demolished hearths in order to avoid the tax. Surviving records date from 1662 to 1674 (Public Record Office and county record offices).

Marriage Registration Tax 1694/5 quickly followed the Hearth Tax and follows the pattern, to a certain extent, of the later ten-yearly census returns in that it showed family groupings. The Act was a tax on births, marriages, bachelors, burials, and childless widowers. Besides being a tax, it also provided the authorities with a census of the population. The Act was repealed in 1706. (County Record Offices).

Poll Taxes from medieval times until the late seventeenth century. These were personal taxes on all those over 16 years of age and not in receipt of poor relief. (County Record Offices and Public Record Office).

Poll Books, as opposed to Poll Taxes, were concerned with elections and voters in county and Parliamentary elections, and can exist up to the latter part of the nineteenth century. They show how an ancestor voted in an election. (County Record Offices, Reference Libraries).

Electoral Registers date from 1832 and are available to the present day. They differ from Poll books by recording all people who were entitled to vote, whether they voted or not. (County Record Offices and Reference Libraries).

The Window Tax was imposed from 1696 to 1851, and this only resulted in householders bricking up their windows in order to evade this unpopular tax. (County Record Offices).

The Land Tax Assessments commenced in 1696 and became perpetual from 1780 lasting until 1831/2. This was a tax on land worth more than twenty shillings and came under the supervision of the County Commissioners. Records give names of occupiers, owners of the land, acreage, type of land and the tax paid. (County Record Offices).

1694 Tax by Parliament on marriages, births, burials, bachelors over 25 years of age and childless widowers dated 1701 for Wroughton, Wiltshire

There are many other records of this kind which not only may be used to trace ancestry back in time, but will corroborate and prove that research is on the correct lines. They can also help to track the whereabouts of a family and its social status at a certain period of time.

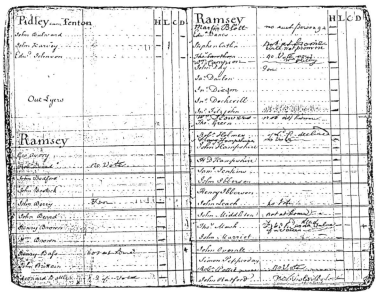

Huntingdonshire — 1790 Poll Book for Ramsey in Hurstingstone Hundred

The ecclesiastical census of 1851

It is worth mentioning that in addition to the 1851 census of the population, another was taken in 1851 on 30 March and this was a census of places of worship. It was arranged by registration districts as in the other census returns, and shows the name and denomination of each place of worship of Anglican churches, non conformist or dissenting Protestant churches and chapels, and Roman Catholic churches.

The returns give the date of consecration or date of the actual building, space available in them for public worship, and totals of attendance at services on 30 March 1851 and the average attendance during the previous year. This census often includes information regarding the buildings and any endowments and may contain various comments by the minister.

Although this census is often ignored by the family historian, it can be of tremendous help in establishing a non-conformist place of worship within a parish and a starting date for any registers or records which may have survived.

Some of the comments and information supplied by the minister may even produce 'family' names!

Next step

Just as the details from a birth, marriage and death certificate obtained from Civil registration give facts and dates which enable one to go on to census returns, so the returns supply detailed information which permit the researcher to proceed to the next stage in tracing their family history. These are parish registers and bishops transcripts.

The information needed from a census return is: Forename or Christian name, surname, age, address, and the county and place of birth with the year of the census.

For example: John Smith aged 45 years at the time of the 1871 census, living at King St. Leighton, Yorks. States he was born at Hungerford, Berkshire.

With John Smith's age deducted from the year of the census, go on to look at the parish registers for Hungerford, Berkshire around the date of 1826, the approximate date of birth.

Comments

- Although the rule in the 1841 census was to round down ages for adults to the nearest five years, occasionally ages for elderly people may have been rounded down to the nearest ten years.
- Take all family details from every census year from 1841 through to 1881 so that a family pattern can be established and seen as a whole.
- Except for the 1841 census when no relationships were given, the relationships on other census returns are to the head of the household and not to one another.
- If a civil registration certificate falls between census dates, either look for other births in civil registration for brothers or sisters, known as 'collaterals', or look at trade or street directories of the certificate date to try and find the family and an address. This method is more helpful if a forbear was a tradesman, in business, or in a profession, but it is always worth trying anyway.
- If unable to find an address on a census, bear in mind that street names and numbers may have changed between the date on your records and the date of the census. Consult a local directory or street map of the locality around the date you are searching. These should be available in a local reference library or record office.
- Whenever a family is found on the census return, wind back the reel to the beginning of that section for a description of the area covered by the enumerator.
- Take your time in the census room — 'make haste slowly' — do not rush and make mistakes which will cost you time and money in the long run. Learn to read the census rather than just look!
- When using the census rooms and microfilm reels, always wind back the reel to the beginning when finished so that it is ready for the next user. When not using the microfilm reader for a while, switch off to avoid over-heating and damage to the film.

Further reading

Census Returns on Microfilm 1841–1881 by J.S.W. Gibson (FFHS).

Marriage, Census and other Indexes for the Family Historian by J.S.W. Gibson
Census Returns 1841–1881 by Eve McLaughlin (FFHS).
Index to Census Registration Districts by M.E. Bryant Rosier and J.K. Marfleet.
Land Tax Assessments c., 1690 to 1950. J.S.W. Gibson and Dennis Mills (FFHS).
The Hearth Tax Other later Stuart Tax Lists and the Association Oath Rolls by J.S.W. Gibson (FFHS).

CHAPTER 4

Parish Registers

In a mandate issued in 1538, Thomas Cromwell, Vicar General to Henry VIII, ordered the clergy to keep records of baptisms, marriages and burials. The response in many cases was cool to say the least. After further prompting from the authorities over the following twenty years, the system eventually improved and most churches kept at least reasonable records of these events.

Over the centuries, the registers have been subject to much abuse by mice, damp, thieves, and general neglect. There are many horror stories around about curates' wives using the parchments for kettle holders, and church officials wrapping meat in them. Needless to say, many are now missing and others are incomplete.

Some clergymen were very conscientious about keeping records, others were not so. Many made little notes in the margins, and some of these gems, give us today an insight of social conditions in the past. One such entry which comes to mind is, 'Mary Lambert brought the child to church herself. Her husband, a worthless man, being too idle to come with her. He applies the same enthusiasm to earning a living as well'. Mr. Lambert was evidently not very well thought of by the Vicar.

In some of the early registers the entries are in Latin, but don't let this deter you, it is usually of a simple variety, and one can soon become adept at translating with aid of a cheap Latin word book.

Where
The Parochial Registers and Record Measures Act, passed in 1978, stated that although the parish records are the property of the Parochial Church Council of the particular parish, they should deposit in the Diocesan Record Office all completed registers over 100 years old. They can be kept at the church only under strict conditions concerning the correct environment to aid preservation. This Act has ensured that the vast majority of parish records are now in the safe keeping of County Record Offices.

Yaxley, Cambridgeshire, Composite Parish Register (1653-1812) for Baptisms, Burials (and Marriages to 1754)

The ones that are still in the churches can be viewed by arrangement with the Vicar, who is entitled to charge the appropriate fees laid down in the Parochial Fees Order, which is adjusted from time to time. Most of the County Record Offices make no charge for viewing the registers in their charge. In many cases it is still possible to see the original volumes, but gradually these

Yaxley Baptism Register 1755 in Composite Register (1653-1812) Marriages to 1754

are being made available on microfiche, due to the condition some of the registers are now in, owing to being handled, at times very carelessly, by researchers. Microform copies are often available in local county libraries too. Many of the registers have been copied and can be seen in such places as the Society of Genealogists' Library in London as well as County Record Offices. Some transcriptions have even found their way as far as Australia and the United States of America.

There are differences between the dates on certificates obtained from civil repositories and the ones gleaned from the parish records. The birth certificate should give the precise date of birth, whilst the date in the church records is usually that of the baptism. The length of time that has elapsed between the birth and the christening varies from a few days old to adulthood; in some cases babies were not christened at all. Many parents had what are often called 'batch baptisms' — this is when the whole family, of perhaps six children, varying in age from a few weeks to say 12 or 13 years old, were all baptized in one ceremony. So don't assume that an entry in a baptism register is the correct date of birth.

Whilst the dates of marriage in church records will, or should, be correct, the dates of death certificates will be different from the ones recorded in the parish records, as the latter will be the dates of the burial ceremonies.

How

As with the civil returns, the parish registers should be searched in a methodical manner. The best approach is to go armed with a good supply of note paper and a pencil. The use of pens is frowned upon in the copying of records, this is to ensure that any slips can be rubbed out.

You may find that you have to travel a great distance to reach the record office, and you have only a limited number of hours in which to do your research, so it follows that no time should be wasted at all.

If you start with the latest records available and work backwards, copying every entry of the name or names you require, this will ensure that no stone is unturned. Another important point to remember is to make a complete copy of the entry, no matter how many seemingly superfluous words there are connected with it. Also, you should make a note to remind yourself from which volume you obtained that particular information.

You will feel most annoyed, if, in two years time, you wish to check an entry and you have no idea from whence it came in the first place.

If you have a relatively uncommon name it is possible that you may be able to complete your search of the registers in one day. However, having said that, it is important not to hurry the work, to do so is a recipe for disaster. Even if it means further visits in the future, take your time and do it right.

Format

In the very early volumes the entries are usually brief, e.g. 'John, the son of John Smith was buried'. As time went by, more details were often added, such as 'John, the son of John Smith and his wife, Mary, was buried'. The extra name added to the second example makes the world of difference, because not only do you know the name of the deceased's father, but you also learn the name of his mother. Usually in the early days, the baptism, marriage and burials entries were recorded in the same book, perhaps the baptisms in the front section, the marriages in the middle and the burials at the end, sometimes interspaced. By 1813, printed books were in use, and the various entries made in separate books giving much more useful information to the researcher. Illustrations of the various types of format accompany this chapter.

Bishops' Transcripts

From the year 1598, it became the recognized practice for the incumbent to send to his local Bishop a full year's copy of the parish register. This event occurred each Easter. These copies are known as the Bishops' Transcripts or BTs.

As with any other copied record, the accuracy of the transcription depends on the capability of the transcriber. Some BTs are a true record of the PRs and some are not. The value of these records lies in their ability to, at times, enable the researcher to fill in gaps in the parish registers which have appeared since the time the original BTs were copied.

Whenever possible, double check BT entries against the original parish register records. Unfortunately BTs are not nearly so complete as PRs and do have many missing years. They extend to the late nineteenth century.

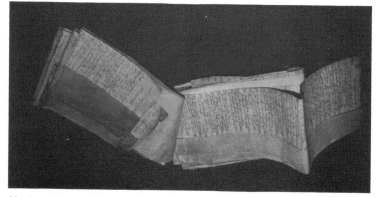

Yaxley Bishops' Transcript Roll open at 1735

The meaning and variations of surnames

The custom of surnames developed in medieval times about the twelfth and thirteenth centuries in England when our forbears only used one name for identification. From this period onwards, surnames gradually became hereditary, starting with the nobility and spreading to the common man in town and country during the next two centuries because of a need for more identification other than being called John son of John, Thomas the cooper, William with the red hair or Michael who lives by the muddy ford.

The practice of surnames in Scotland and Ireland followed somewhat later than in England and in Wales, hereditary surnames were not finally adopted

Yaxley Bishops' Transcripts. Close up of the page illustrated above

until well into the late eighteenth and early nineteenth centuries.

Surnames fall into four broad categories:

1. Surnames based on a first name, male or female, such as Johnson/Johnstone meaning John, son of John; Goodson, son of Good; Emms, son of Emma; Dickenson, son of Dicken (a pet name for Richard).
2. Surnames based on a place or locality from where an ancestor had originated. For example, Lydiard (places in Wiltshire and Somerset); York from Yorkshire; Elstone from Elstone (hamlets in Devon and Wiltshire); Leicester/Lester/Lessiter from Leicester; Coombe, from a small valley; Mudford, by the muddy ford; Parke, by the enclosure or park; Pitman, living at the pit or hollow.
3. Surnames based on a nickname which described an ancestor in some way, either his looks, figure, temperament etc. For example Redhead, red haired; Tench, fat and sleek; Trueman, trusty and faithful; Bragge, proud, arrogant, brisk, brave; Blunt, blond, fair.
4. Surnames which recorded the occupation or status of an ancestor. For example, Parmenter/Parminster, tailor; Dexter, dyer; Neate, ox or cowherd; Cooper, barrel maker; Walker, one who trod on cloth in a trough in the fulling process; Fletcher, arrow maker or seller.

Names have varied immensely over the centuries with dialect, intonation, and often an inability to spell on the part of parish clerks, and illiteracy on the part of our ancestors. In fact, it was not until the late nineteenth century and the Education Act of 1870 that some kind of stability came to surnames, establishing them as we spell them today.

Variation in surname spelling must be taken into consideration at all times by the family historian when commencing research into a family. It may even be found that surnames vary in spelling from one branch of the family to the next.

For instance, V and F can be interchangeable as in Fosse and Vosse or Volkes and Folkes. An 'H' may be put in front of a name such as Alford or Elford making it into Halford or Helford. Letters may be added to or taken from a surname, and the dialect of an ancestral county must be considered when searching for a name.

The West country family of Phillips varied in spelling in the past from Philipe to Philpe to Phelps and even to Filp back in the 1500s and the standard 'Phillips' as it is spelt today only became stable in the late 1800s.

An unusual surname can often be traced through telephone directories to find where today's families are located. There is an organization called the Guild of One Name Studies (GOONS) which brings together under one banner all those studying a certain surname, and it is a good idea to check with this society to find if anyone else is collecting all references and information referring to your surname. Fuller details may be found in Chapter 14.

It is always wise to find out if anyone else has done any work in the past on your surname and family. There may be historical references, notes, or even books written about some families and these may prove to be of help with research. Names may be found in the various Genealogists Guides and there are also directories of others researching surnames in a particular locality and for a certain period of time, and it is worthwhile looking at these shortly after you have made a start on your family research when you have established a few names, dates, places and generations.

The Commonwealth

After the death of King Charles I in 1649, England went through the period popularly known as the Commonwealth. Many clergymen at this time opposed Oliver Cromwell's rule, and there was a great deal of friction between the two bodies. Much of this was reflected in the keeping of parish records. In 1653 the responsibility passed to a person who was paid one shilling for doing the work. This could have been anyone from the parish who was capable of filling in the entries. It did not matter much whether he was an able book-keeper or not. As a consequence, once again we have a period when record keeping was very unstable. Some of the records kept during that time are to be found in County Record Offices; they are very well compiled and often give more information than the earlier ones. Regretfully, many are missing altogether.

During this time of unrest, from 1653-1660, a kind of civil registration of marriages was instituted. Banns were no longer read in church, and no licences were issued but the intention to marry was announced on three occasions in a public place, and the marriage ceremony was then performed by a JP or an authorized minister.

When Royalty was restored in 1660, the system was reverted back to the pre-Commonwealth times. Some clergymen took the trouble to keep the continuity of the registers, others went the opposite way and destroyed the Commonwealth records.

Banns

Banns are another useful source of information found in the parish register. The general rule was, and still is, that couples wishing to be married in church had banns of their intention to marry read on three occasions in the parish church of both the bride and groom.

Banns are particularly useful for finding out which parish a bride or groom lived in, other than the one you are searching at the present time. For example, if you knew John Simpson lived in Newtown parish in the days before so much detail appeared on the marriage entries, and if you can find a copy of the banns which were recorded before the ceremony, this will inform you of exactly which parish his bride-to-be lived, where incidentally most of the marriages took place.

Yaxley Banns Register 1834/5

Non-conformists

This word means really what it says. They were people who did not conform to the pattern of the established church. Some examples of these are the Catholics, Jews, Quakers, Methodists and Baptists. There were many more of course. Other popular names used for some of these people were dissenters and recusants.

If your family seems suddenly to vanish from parish records in the area you are researching, it is most likely for one of two reasons. The first is that they lived in another area, and the second is that perhaps they could have been non-conformists. If you suspect that they belonged to the latter group, the task then is to try to locate the registers of such bodies.

The Quakers and Jews were allowed to marry within their respective churches, and both groups still hold their own records.

Roman Catholics were very much repressed by the established church. They were fined for not attending Anglican services, and for attending Catholic ones. For many years the Catholic church became something of an underground society. Baptisms and marriages continued in secret, but to keep within the law the services were repeated in the Anglican church. It was only possible to be buried in the parish church. From the Hardwicke Marriage Act of 1754 only marriages in the Anglican church were legal. Beginning in 1778 the stringent laws were relaxed, and by 1791 Roman Catholics were, at last, officially allowed to worship in their own churches.

Here we have dealt with parish registers and have not covered the wealth of other parish records that are available to the researcher. The church was responsible for many other day-to-day functions in times past. (see Chapters 7 and 8).

Yaxley Parish Registers
Marriage entry in Composite Register (1653-1812 Marriages to 1754)
open at Marriages 1727.
See marriage licence bond of Josiah Smith to Mary Howes both of
Glatton, 29 June 1727 to marry at Yaxley Church.

Marriage licences, bonds and allegations

If a marriage entry in a register appears with 'by licence' against it then a search should be made for the licence bond or allegation. The licence itself was usually given to the minister by the couple marrying and so has not always survived, although there are instances where some were placed in the Parish Chest (see Chapter 7).

The licence bond or allegation will give information of value, as it will show those who stood surety for the licence, sometimes up to the sum of £200, as well as the names of the bride and groom, together with the groom's mark or signature, and, at times, where the marriage was supposed to take place. Quite often occupations are also shown for the sureties and the groom.

It was usual for gentry and the yeoman class to marry by licence; after all, they did not particularly want the 'hoi polloi' knowing all about their affairs by having banns 'called' in the parish church. In some families it was a tradition to be married by licence. If a working or labouring class couple wanted to marry on a fast day, Holy day or in Lent, they too, had to apply for a licence to marry.

No licences were issued during the Commonwealth period from 1653 to 1660 when all marriage ceremonies were civil ones. Licences were granted from the fourteenth century, but usually only exist from the sixteenth/ seventeenth centuries onwards. They were issued by the Bishop, Dean, the Archbishop's office, and occasionally by other ecclesiastical officials. They will be found in county record offices or diocesan record offices, or in the records of the Archbishop.

Acts of parliament relating to parish registers

Burial in Wool Acts of 1667 and 1678

These acts stated that all corpses should be buried in wool, except those who had died from the plague. The 1678 Act in particular stated that 'no corpse of any person shall be buried in any shirt, shift, sheet or shroud or anything

Yaxley Burial Register 1741 in Composite Register (1653-1812) Marriages to 1754

whatsoever made or mingled with flax, hemp, silk, hair, gold or silver, or in any stuff or thing other than what is made of sheep's wool only'. An affidavit was required to be sworn within a few days of the burial that the deceased had indeed been buried in woollen only and this was duly recorded in the burial register. If a burial in woollen had not taken place there was a fine of £5. Burials in wool gradually fell into disuse and by 1814 the acts were repealed.

Lord Chesterfield's Act 1751-52
This was an act to change the calendar from the Julian calendar, which commenced on the 25th March on Ladyday each year until the following 24th March, to the Gregorian calendar which began on the 1st January to the 31st December each year.

This act stated that the year 1752 would commence on 1 January until 31 December, but for that particular year only, to adjust the calendar for all time, 2 September was to be followed by 14 September thus omitting eleven days.

The Hardwicke Marriage Act 1754
Sooner or later you will come across references to the Hardwicke Marriage Act. This was introduced in 1754. Before that date 'Clandestine Marriages' were not unlawful. There were marriages which, although the participants had not fully obeyed the letter of the law, were not invalidated.

On the introduction of the Act on 25 March, 1754, all marriages had to be recorded in a separate book and no longer with the births and deaths. The entries had to show the place of residence of both parties and their marital status, and had to be signed by the bride, groom, and two or more witnesses. Also marriages were not allowed to be performed in any church other than the parish church: the Quakers and Jews being the only exceptions.

The introduction of this act was designed to end marriages in such places as prison chapels, public houses, and the premises of minor houses of religion; even the Catholic Church was not allowed to carry out lawful marriage ceremonies.

Stamp Act of 1783
A duty of 3d was imposed on all entries in the parish register, baptisms, marriages and burials, with the minister receiving a commission from this revenue. A most unpopular tax which was repealed in 1794.

The Rose or Parochial Registers Act 1812-13
In 1813 the George Rose's Act was introduced. This ensured that the parish register entries were laid out in a formal fashion in all parish churches. From this date also each group of entries had its own register.

Parish register changes throughout the centuries
In 1538 at the start of parish registers, baptisms, marriages, and burials were usually together on one page, sometimes mixed although in chronological order.

Marriage Licence bond for Marriage of Josiah Smith of Glatton to Mary Howes of Glatton 29 June 1727 at Yaxley Church. See Marriages Parish Registers Yaxley 1727.

In 1732 registers were ordered to be written in English, and until this time registers may be in Latin, although not usually so.

Baptisms, marriages, and burials during the eighteenth century would be recorded in separate parts of the register, if not in separate registers. Baptismal entries often use only the child's name and father's name at this time, not the mother. By the end of the eighteenth century, however, most clergymen had started to add the mother's christian name to the entry in the baptismal register.

Marriage Licence for Henry Gray of St Ann, Blackfriars, London and Mary Gray of Yaxley, Huntingdon. 4 June 1819. Vicar General — Archbishop of Canterbury.

From 1754 all marriages had to be entered in an especially printed register. The information given was parish of origin of bride and groom, whether spinster, bachelor or widow(er); signatures or marks of bride and groom; signatures or marks of two witnesses or more, and whether the marriage had taken place by banns or licence. If the marriage was by 'banns' the record would be made either in a separate Banns Book, at the top of the marriage entry or at the end of the marriage register.

Before 1812 burial entries varied in detail, but from 1813 a printed register was provided, completely separate from the marriage and baptismal registers. Much more information was given about the deceased person.

After 1813, a separate baptismal register was provided and more details were given than previously.

After 1837 and civil registration, marriage registers were altered and include the same information as shown on marriage certificates.

Yaxley Baptism Register 1826 (in use after Rose's Act 1812)

Comments

- No parish registers existed before 1538, and not too many even before the early 1600s.
- Most parish registers are now in county record offices; however, some may still be at the church. Check the present whereabouts with the county record

Yaxley Burial Register 1842 (in use after Rose's Act 1812)

and *Elizabeth Burnett* .... of *this* Parish

were married in this *Church* by *Banns* with Consent of
_____ this *5th* _____ Day of
February in the Year One thousand eight hundred and *37*
.... By me *John Spurway Recta*
This Marriage was solemnized between us { *Benmark of* † *William Rew*
In the Presence of { *the mark of* † *Eliz Rew*
{ *R Thailand*
No. 850. *W Haplighmark* †

_____ *Thomas Daw Richard* of *this* Parish

and *Mary Ann* _____ *Archer* .... of *this* Parish

were married in this *Church* by *Banns* with Consent of
_____ this *5th* _____ Day of
February in the Year One thousand eight hundred and *37*
.... By me *John Spurway Recta*
This Marriage was solemnized between us { *Benmark of* †
In the Presence of { *the mark of* † *Mary Ann* ☒
{ *R Thailand*
No. 851.

George Phillips _____ Parish

and *Mary Ann Foss both Sojns in this* Parish

were married in this *Church* by *Banns* with Consent of
_____ this *Twelfth* _____ Day of
February in the Year One thousand eight hundred and *Thirty Seven*
By me *Wm Loksg Littg*
This Marriage was solemnized between us { *the mark* ☒ *of George Phillips*
{ *Mary Ann Foss*

Marriage Register (1837). Tiverton St. Peter Devon

office concerned before making any journeys.
- A date on a baptism entry is not the date of birth and that on a burial entry is not the date of death.
- In 1752 a change was made from the Julian calendar to the Gregorian. Under the old system the year began on 25 March so records often read in the manner 1701/2. After the changeover the year began on 1 January. Another point to remember is that for reckoning the year before 1752 try to think that the months of January, February, and March to the 24th, were the end of the year; the new year commencing on 25 March.

- Always check any Bishop's Transcript entries with the originals in the parish registers wherever possible.
- If there is a gap in the parish register entries try to find the Bishop's Transcripts to help fill it in.
- Be very wary of variants, different spellings of the same surname.
- Check for existence of banns, these are a very useful source of information especially so if your ancestor married in another parish.
- Check non-conformist records where available.
- Baptisms may not always be at the time of a child's birth but several weeks, months, or years afterwards. Check for adult baptisms, especially at the time of the Stamp Duty Act of 1783 which lasted until 1794, when the numbers of baptisms declined and the numbers of paupers rose in an endeavour to evade this tax.
- Sometimes a child may have been baptized more than once — in an Anglican church and a non-conformist chapel.
- The marriage age was 14 years for a male and 12 years for a female with consent of parents or guardians until the full age of twenty-one years was reached. This 'marriage age' continued, even after the 1754 Hardwicke Marriage Act, until 1929 when a new act raised the marriage age to 16 years for both sexes, with consent of parents or guardians until 21 years of age.

Further reading

Parish Registers by Eve McLaughlin (FFHS).
Simple Latin by Eve McLaughlin (FFHS).
Record Offices: How to find them by Jeremy Gibson and Pamela Peskett (FFHS).
London Local Archives (Greater London Archives Network and Guildhall Library).
Bishops Transcripts and Marriage Licences by Jeremy Gibson (FFHS).
Marriage Indexes by J.S.W. Gibson (FFHS).
Atlas and Index of Parish Registers, ed. by Cecil Humphery-Smith (Phillimore).
Parish Chest by W.E. Tate (Phillimore).
Dictionary of British Surnames by P.H. Reaney (RKP 1983).
The Origin of English Surnames by P.H. Reaney (RKP 1984).
Surnames by Basil Cottle (Penguin 1977).
A Dictionary of English and Welsh Surnames by C.W. Bardsley (Gen Pub. Co. Baltimore 1980 and Heraldry Today, London).
The Genealogist's Guide by G.W. Marshall (Heraldry Today 1973).
A Genealogical Guide by J.B. Whitmore (Walford Bros. London 1953).
Genealogist's Guide by G.B. Barrow (Research Pub. Co. London 1977).
A Catalogue of British Family Histories ed. by T.R. Thomson (Research Pub. Co. London. 3rd. ed. 1980).

CHAPTER 5

Non-Conformists and their Records

The evolution of non-conformity in this country was extremely complex, and therefore it is necessary to put the reader 'in the picture' by giving a rather detailed history of the subject so that it may be understood in the context of researching a family history.

If a family cannot be found in the Church of England parish registers and bishop's transcripts, or, if a family have wholly disappeared from sight and all surrounding parishes and parish records have been searched, then it may well be possible that the family had left the Anglican church in favour of a non-conformist or dissenting sect. On occasion it is likely that a family worshipped and had their children christened and buried in more than one denomination. Many people discovered that certain sects held more attraction in the way they preached the Christian message and the gospel than the established Church of England.

Every researcher must keep an open mind on this subject and search the records of non-conformists if a family has been 'lost' from the parish registers. It is also possible that families may return to the Church of England at certain periods during their lifetimes and those of their children.

The history of non-conformity

Non-Conformity was the religious movement implying dissent from the established church and was the attitude of all Christian bodies that did not conform to the Church of England.

Protestantism was the religious doctrine or principles of Protestants, and this term was coined after the protest made by Martin Luther and his followers in 1529 against what they thought were the intolerant decisions of the Roman Catholic Church. Gradually, the word Protestant came to describe the churches and people who severed their connection with Rome at the time of the Reformation.

The Reformation movement started with Martin Luther in 1517 at Wittenburg in Germany when he denounced Pope Leo X's sale of indulgences. This revolution followed in varying degrees in Europe, but in England about this time Henry VIII decided to refute Luther's heresies and in return he was rewarded by the Pope with the title of 'Defender of the Faith', still shown on our coinage to this day.

However, by 1533, Henry had been excommunicated by the Pope from the Roman Catholic Church because of his continued defiance in trying to divorce his unwanted wife Catherine (of Aragon) in order to marry Anne Boleyn and beget, he hoped, a male heir for the throne of England, and so continue the Tudor dynasty.

In 1534 Henry VIII declared himself 'Supreme Head of the English Church' by the Act of Supremacy and the rift with the Catholic Church and Rome was finally complete. This resulted in two factions and disunity within the church in this country. Firstly, there were the parish priests who decided to accept Henry as Supreme Head of the Church, and who continued to perform the ceremonies of christenings, marriages and burials of their congregations as usual. These eventually formed the nucleus of the Church of England as we know it today. On the other hand, there were the parish priests who refused to accept Henry as the Supreme Head, and who still followed the teachings and rites of the Church of Rome, together with many of their parishioners.

Gradually, around 1563, Roman Catholics started to keep their own records of baptisms, marriages and burials, although many of these records were lost or destroyed through the various harassments of the seventeenth and eighteenth centuries. As the reign of James I (1603-1625) progressed, other groups, referred to as Puritans or Dissenters, came into prominence and it was by these names that they were known until the Act of Uniformity in 1662. This act required all ministers to assent to everything contained in, and prescribed by, the Book of Common Prayer, known as the Thirty-nine Articles. Some 2,000 ministers who did not agree were ejected from their livings in the Church of England.

Dissenting chapels were set up all over the country for those who held a variety of beliefs which at this time were described as Independents. Those who did not believe in episcopacy (the government of the church by bishops) were known as Presbyterians, and Separatists. Who believed that Congregationalism (a system of Church government that gave independence to each local church) was the only basis for a Christian church.

Members of the Society of Friends (or Quakers) avoided all ritual in their worship and believed that every individual had power of direct communication with God. Their worship was maintained in silence until someone was moved by the Holy Spirit to utter his message. The term 'Quaker' was first used by their founder, George Fox, who bade a judge 'Quake ye before the Lord'.

Baptists were Independents who objected to infant baptism, and Unitarians rejected the doctrine of the Trinity (union in one Godhead of the Father, Son and Holy Ghost). The beliefs of this last sect were illegal until 1813.

Dissenting chapels were known as Conventicles, and the Conventicle Act of 1664 made it a penal offence to attend their services. The Five Mile Act of 1665 prohibited such ministers from preaching within five miles of any town and also barred them from keeping schools.

Despite all these tribulations, meetings were held in secret and the numbers of non-conformists or dissenters gradually increased. The 'Glorious Revolution' of 1688 overthrew Roman Catholic James II from the throne of England and sent him into exile. William of Orange and his wife Mary acceded to the throne early in 1689. The Toleration Act of 1689 gave religious freedom to all who accepted thirty-six out of the Thirty-nine Articles of religion, and from this time relief came to non-conformist churches, as the Act enabled Protestant dissenters to practise their own forms of worship in premises licensed for that purpose and did away with penalties for disobedience. These provisions for registering houses, in the Toleration Act of 1689, remained until 1812 — although in 1791 another act did extend to Roman Catholics some of the benefits of toleration. A new Toleration Act in 1812 made many alterations to the procedures for registering meeting houses, and registration became compulsory for any religious assembly 'at which there shall be present more than 20 persons, besides the immediate family and servants of the person in whose house or upon whose premises' meetings took place. Certificates of meeting houses are to be found in county record offices dating from 1689 to around 1852, and dissenting ministers' or teachers' oaths and declarations from 1689 onwards until about 1829 are to be found there as well, in the records of the Clerk of the Peace. By 1832, Roman Catholics were, at last, allowed to have their own places of worship.

In 1836, at the same time that Civil registration of births, marriages and deaths was being introduced into England and Wales there was the establishment of a Royal Commission, and non-Anglican (Protestant) churches were invited to send their registers to the Registrar General so that their authenticity could be checked.

Many registers, but not all, were submitted and a list of deposited registers was published in 1841. In 1857, a second request was made for registers to be sent in, and a list of these was published in 1859. All non-parochial registers and records submitted are now in the Public Record Office at Chancery Lane, London. It must be noted that Roman Catholics and Jews, in the main, declined to submit their registers. However, some early registers which were not submitted to the Registrar General have now found their way into county record offices, and non-conformist libraries, whilst others may still be in the hands of their ministers.

The Marriage Act of 1836 empowered Superintendent Registrars to issue licences for marriage in the office of a registrar or in a non-conformist church. After 1 July 1837 any non-conformist church or chapel which had been open for a year could apply for its premises to be licensed for marriages. If a licence was granted, the registrar attended with his marriage register, registered the marriage and took the register back with him to the Register Office.

Extract from '*Original Records of Early Non-Conformists under Persecution and Indulgence'* (3 Vols). From returns of conventicles or meeting houses in Episcopal Returns dated 1669:-

Sarum (Salisbury Diocese)
Bremble, Wilts.
Where:- At ye house of Widdow Hales. *Sect:* Quakers.
Number: 300 or 400 sometime.
Quality and Abettors: Meane people and ignorant. *Teachers:* A wandering Teacher out of ye North sometimes, but more neere, Wm. Hand an un-learned schoolmaster and Humphery Oliffe an illiterate surgeon.
Archdeaconry of Sarum (Salisbury)
Atworth, Wilts.
Where: At Sam'l Loves house. *Sect:* Anabaptists. *Number:* 20 or 30.
Quality and Abettors: Meane quality. *Teachers:* One Painter of Wrexall (Wraxall), silkman and Sam'l Loves, aforesaid, flockman.

The above abstracts from these returns of non-conformist conventicles or meeting houses at this period in time — 1669, shows the low regard in which dissenters were held by the established Church of England.

Non-parochial registers in the Public Record Office, Chancery Lane, London

The following list comprises the main non-conformist sects and their registers deposited in the Public Record Office for England and Wales. The exception is the register of the Independent Church at St. Petersburg in Russia dating from 1818 to 1840. There are registers for other minor sects and it is suggested that when ancestry has been established in a certain county, the registers for the particular area in which ancestry lies should be consulted. In all, some 7,000 volumes and files under the grouping of the Registrar General (RG) are in the Public Record Office (see Chapter 13).

Where are they now?

Non-conformist registers which were not deposited in the Public Record Office may have subsequently found their way into the county record office collection. Some, however, may still be in the possession of the minister of the particular sect. If this last is the case the archivist of the county record office should be able to supply the minister's name and address.

Baptists

Although the first church in England dated from 1612, the earliest known registers date from 1647. Many other archives are to be found at Baptist Church House, Southampton Row, London, WC13 4AB, and at Dr. William's Library, 14 Gordon Square, London WC1E 0AG.

Congregationalists

One of the earliest dissenting denominations, the first known date for registers is for London in 1644. Other records are now administered by Dr. William's Library.

Baptismal Register of the Congregational Church, Old George Yard, Kimbolton, Huntingdonshire dated 1809

Some Congregational churches did not join the United Reformed Church in 1972 and have remained independent from this organization, comprising the Congregational Federation.

Huguenots

Initially a name coined for French Protestants but was also bestowed on other Protestants in the Low Countries. Many Huguenots fled from persecution to other Protestant countries including England during the reigns of Henry VIII and Edward VI and settled in places such as London, Norwich, Plymouth and Canterbury where they were gradually absorbed into the English community. Some of their records date from 1567 although other records go back to the early sixteenth century. The registers were deposited with the Registrar General but the Huguenot Society has published most of the registers as well as other Huguenot records.

Methodists

This name was synonymous with the Wesley brothers, John and Charles. It is necessary to realize that at one time Methodism was split into various factions — for instance, Wesleyan, Bible Christian, Primitive Methodist, New Connexion, Tent Methodists, and so on. By 1932 most of these had joined together to become the Methodist Church. The earliest registers date from around 1779 for London, 1780 for Somerset, and 1784 for Lancashire.

St. Ives, Huntingdonshire Methodist Circuit Baptismal Register — entry dated 1863

Moravians

The Moravian church started in London and Oxford about 1723, and in 1742 the congregation of the Unity of the Brethren was founded. The earliest registers date from 1741 for London, 1742 for Yorkshire and 1743 for Bedfordshire. Some of these registers date up to 1754, the date of the Hardwicke Marriage Act, and include marriages as well as baptisms and burials.

The Society of Friends (Quakers)

Founded in 1647 by George Fox, the Friends underwent many persecutions for their faith. In the 1650s the Society of Friends in London started keeping records. Quakers were exempt from the Hardwicke Marriage Act 1754, and were still allowed to marry within their own faith and not in the Church of England.

These records are the most comprehensive of all the registers and were transcribed before being deposited with the Registrar General. There is an index to the registers available at the Society of Friends Library, Friends House, Euston Road, London. A charge is made for the use of the library.

United Reformed Church

This church was founded in 1972 and is the successor to the Presbyterian and Independent, subsequently the Congregational churches.

Presbyterian

These registers are deposited in the Public Record Office, the earliest dating from 1650 for York, 1672 for Devon and 1676 for Cheshire. Dr. Williams' Library also has records of Presbyterian chapels.

A selection of some other non-parochial registers in the Public Record Office

- Bible Christian
- Calvinist Methodist
- Countess of Huntingdon's Connection
- Inghamite or the Catholic Apostolic church
- Irvingite
- Lutheran (London)
- New Jerusalemite or Swedenborgian
- Unitarian
- Some Foreign Protestant churches in Britain.

Very few Roman Catholic registers were deposited, and those which were refer mainly to the north of England. Other Roman Catholic registers and records are still usually in the custody of the 'priest in charge' of the parish.

The Catholic Record Society has published some registers and other historical records dating from the sixteenth century. Occasionally some registers or microfilm of registers may be discovered in county record offices.

Jewish records

These were never deposited with the Registrar General but should be either with the synagogues or possibly in some county record offices. It must be noted that Jews were banished from England in 1290 and only re-admitted during the Commonwealth in 1655.

Two classes of Jews came into Britain — the Sephardic Jews from Portugal, Italy, and Spain, and the Ashkenazi Jews from Eastern Europe, Holland and Germany. Many migrated to escape the pogroms in eastern Europe in the late 1800s and again in the 1930s from Nazi Germany, making their way to this country and other safe countries.

Mormons (The Church of Jesus Christ of Latterday Saints)

See Chapter 9 on Mormons and the International Genealogical Index.

Miscellaneous records with the Non-Parochial Records

Although these records are in the Public Record Office, they are not strictly non-parochial records, but are of value to the genealogist.

Cemetery Records

There were a number of non-conformist cemeteries such as Bunhill Fields, London, the Bethnal Green (Gibraltar) burial ground, London, and some other burial grounds.

Hospital Registers

These are registers of the British Lying-in Hospital, Holborn, Chelsea, Foundling and Greenwich hospitals.

Prison Registers

Prison registers for the Fleet and the King's Bench Prison with records of baptisms and marriages from 1647 to 1756. There are registers for other places in London — Mayfair and the Mint, Southwark, (see Chapter 12, Projects and Indexes).

Dr. Williams' library

Dr. Daniel Williams, who died in 1716, was a Presbyterian minister, who in later years developed Unitarian views. On his death his collection of books and manuscripts were bequeathed for public use and a library was opened known as 'The Dissenters' Library'. The contents of this library, together with other donations, are in the Library at Gordon Square in London. The collection covers, in general, the history of non-conformity in England. The library includes a card index of all Congregationalist ministers, and there are copies of the Congregational Year Book with obituaries of ministers. The library is open from Monday to Friday. (Monday, Wednesday and Friday from 10.00 a.m. to 5 p.m., and on Tuesday and Thursday from 10.00 a.m. to 6.30 p.m.) Apply in the first instance to the Librarian, Dr. Williams' Library, 14 Gordon Square, London, WC1H 0AG.

Comments

- Although many non-conformist registers commenced around 1660 to 1700, the majority do not start until the eighteenth century. These records are generally of births, baptisms, deaths and burials.
- As many non-conformist sects did not have their own burial grounds, burials often took place in Church of England graveyards.
- Parish registers often record early non-conformist events such as a birth or death, referring to them in general terms as 'anabaptists'.
- Before the passing of the Hardwicke Marriage Act 1753/4, it was possible to contract a common-law marriage by making a declaration before witnesses. This kind of marriage was frowned on as being 'irregular' but it was still accepted as a true or valid marriage by the Church and State. Nonconformists could be married in this way in their own meeting houses, but after the Hardwicke Marriage Act all marriages had to be solemnized in the Church of England by a minister of that church. The only exceptions were Jews and Quakers who were still allowed to marry within their own faiths. If marriage registers of non-conformist churches or chapels from 1754 to 1898 are discovered which were not submitted for authentication to the Registrar General and they are not in the Public Record Office then they are not strictly official records in the eyes of the law.
- Many sects 'came and went' from the seventeenth century onwards and any records which did exist may have completely disappeared. However, in county record offices are the 'meeting house certificates' from 1689 to 1852, when the system of registering these houses came to an end. These certificates should be searched for non-conformist ancestry as well as the 1851 ecclesiastical census for evidence of non-conformist chapels.

Further reading

Sources for Roman Catholic and Jewish Genealogy (National Index of Parish Registers Volume 3 Society of Genealogists).

Sources for Non-Conformist Genealogy and Family History (National Index of Parish Registers Vol 2 Society of Genealogists).

My Ancestor was Jewish (Society of Genealogists).

My Ancestor was a Baptist (Society of Genealogists).

My Ancestor was a Methodist (Society of Genealogists).

My Ancestor was a Quaker (Society of Genealogists).

Recusant History — A Journal of Research in Post Reformation Catholic History in the British Isles (The Catholic Record Society Vol. 16 No. 4. 1983).

Understanding the History and Records of Non-conformity by Patrick Palgrave-Moore (Elvery Dowers 1987).

CHAPTER 6

Wills and Administrations (Admons)

Wills and administrations (probate records) before 1858

For the genealogist, wills fall into two periods of time — before and after 1858 when civil district registries were set up in England and Wales for the probate of wills. It was from this time that the power of granting probate was effectually taken away from the church authorities and given to the state. Before 1858 wills and administrations were proved in the ecclesiastical courts.

During the middle ages the complex system of granting probate and administration in the church courts was based on the ecclesiastical court hierarchy and this is how it continued until the State take-over on 11 January 1858.

Probate Jurisdictions

The Archdeacon's Court would have jurisdiction and would normally prove a will or grant letters of administration if the testator's (deceased's) property fell only within the area of the Archdeaconry.

The Bishop's Diocesan Court known as the *Consistory Court* or the *Commissary Court* (part of a Bishop's court) had jurisdiction if the property was held in more than one Archdeaconry.

If the deceased's property was held in more than one diocese then the will would be proved in the *Archbishop's Court*, of which there were two, called Provinces — *The Prerogative Court of Canterbury* and *The Prerogative Court of York*. If, however, the deceased's property fell in more than one province then the *Prerogative Court of Canterbury* as the senior province in the land would prove the will.

The Prerogative Court of York, also known as the PCY, covered counties up to the Scottish borders — namely, Cheshire, Durham, part of Flintshire, Lancashire, Northumberland, Nottinghamshire, Westmorland, Yorkshire and the Isle of Man, with wills and administrations dating from 1389 to 1858.

Lastly, there were *Peculiars*, the smallest jurisdictions or courts of all. These could cover one or more parishes such as a manorial court, city, town or university. Peculiars were often quite widely spread and were exempt from the authority of the Archdeacon and often from the Bishop's jurisdiction.

It must be noted, however, that many of these Peculiar Courts had not functioned long before the Probate Act of 1857 came into effect.

Last Will and Testament

The Statute of Wills in 1540 provided that a *Will* dealt with real estate (realty), i.e. property, land and buildings, and a *Testament* dealt with personal property (personalty), i.e. goods, chattles, personal belongings, money, tools, crops, furniture and leases. Gradually, as time went on these two terms became interchangeable and came to have the same meaning. Church courts had no jurisdiction over real estate at all, only leases, and a man had to have goods to the value of £5 or more, known as 'bona notabilia', in one jurisdiction for his will to go to probate.

A *Will* is the final statement and desire of a person and in this important document will be found true statements as to the last bequests and wishes of the deceased.

Letters of Administration also known as '*Admons*' were a grant of probate to the next of kin or other suitable adults over the age of twenty-one years where no will was left and where the next of kin desired to administer the estate. Again, it must be noted that an admon, as well as a will, had to have goods to the value of £5 or more before probate would be granted.

Administration was granted where the deceased had not left a will, this was known as dying 'intestate'. In cases where a will did not specify an executor or an executrix to administer the will or where an executor was unable, or in some cases unwilling, to act, then the court would grant Letters of Administration to the next of kin or other persons who had applied to the court to administer the deceased's estate.

For the family historian a will is an invaluable document, often pre-dating parish registers, and may even date back to the fourteenth century. It is evidence and proof of a family structure and can authenticate births, baptisms, marriages, deaths, burials and family relationships, and can provide proof that research is correct. No other document gives quite the same information as a will and it is this record which speaks from the past. It gives an indication as to how affairs stood within the family from a husband to his wife, children, grandchildren, and kinsfolk, and it itemized in detail the way an ancestor wanted his estate and affairs settled. Obviously, not every person left a will, and an administration was not taken out for everyone who died intestate, but for those who did, they can be a boon to the researcher. Legally, a will had to be made by a testator, often shortly before death. It named beneficiaries, executors and witnesses (witnesses were not allowed to benefit from the will), often with a place of burial and an address.

Verbal death bed utterances were acceptable in law provided they were attested to by three witnesses and provided that the testator had been resident in the place where he died for ten days or more. Usually, these death

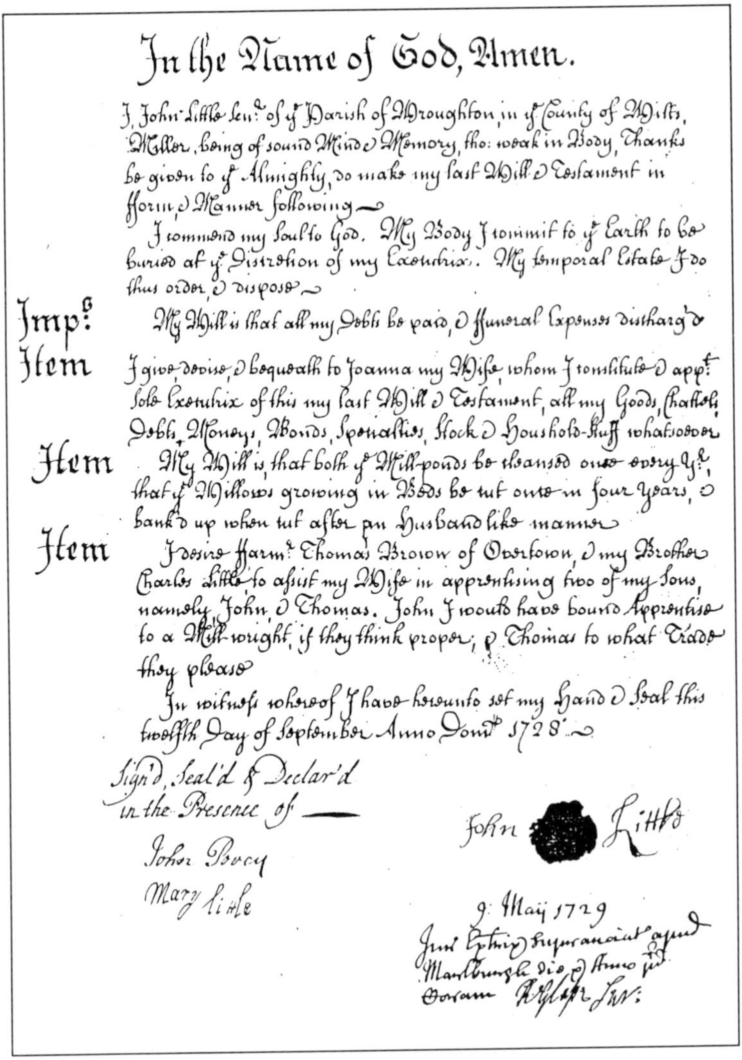

The image below shows a handwritten will in elaborate 18th-century script.

> In the Name of God, Amen.
>
> I, John Little, Sen.ʳ of y.ᵉ Parish of Wroughton in y.ᵉ County of Wilts, Miller, being of sound Mind & Memory, tho: weak in Body, Thanks be given to y.ᵉ Almighty, Do make my last Will & Testament in form & Manner following —
>
> I commend my Soul to God. My Body I commit to y.ᵉ Earth to be buried at y.ᵉ Discretion of my Executrix. My temporal Estate I do thus order & Dispose —

Imp: My Will is that all my Debts be paid, & Funeral Expenses discharg'd

Item I give devise & bequeath to Joanna my Wife, whom I constitute & app.ᵗ sole Executrix of this my last Will & Testament, all my Goods, Chattels, Debts, Moneys, Bonds, Specialties, Stock & Houshold-stuff whatsoever.

Item My Will is, that both y.ᵉ Mill-ponds be cleansed once every y.ᵉ, that y.ᵉ Willows growing in Beds be cut once in four Years, & bank'd up when cut after an Husband-like manner

Item I desire Farm.ʳ Thomas Brown of Overtown, & my Brother Charles Little to assist my Wife in apprenticing two of my Sons, namely, John & Thomas. John I would have bound Apprentice to a Mill-wright, if they think proper; & Thomas to what Trade they please

> In witness whereof I have hereunto set my Hand & Seal this twelfth Day of September Anno Dom.ⁱ 1728 —
>
> Sign'd, Seal'd & Declar'd
> in the Presence of ——
>
> John Bucy
> Mary Little
>
> John ✶ Little
>
> 9. May 1729

Will of John Little, Senior, Miller of Wroughton dated 1728 (Archdeaconry of Wiltshire)

bed wills begin 'memorandum quod' or even just 'memorandum'. Verbal death bed utterances or nuncupative wills, as they were known, were different from a dictated will signed by a testator. Nuncupative wills were abolished by the Wills Act 1836/7 except for those on active service.

In the days when England was wholly Roman Catholic, a man would often leave money for prayers for his soul and for masses to be said in his parish church. Often, too, a sum of money would be left for the poor of the parish, or other bequests for food and clothing for the poor. A man would leave his wife his personal estate with the proviso that she should not re-marry, for if she did, then her portion would revert to the family, as her new husband would by law, automatically own everything of which she was possessed.

From 1540 until 1837 a will could be made by any male over the age of 14 years and by a female over the age of 12 years. After 1837 a testator had to be of full age, that is to say, 21 years or over.

The 1540 Statute of Wills stated that no married woman could make a will, because by law everything she owned on marriage became the property of her husband. Other persons unable to make a will were lunatics, (lunatics' estates were usually a subject of litigation and were dealt with in the Prerogative Court of Canterbury or in Chancery), prisoners, apostates (deserters, renegades) and traitors. It was not until the Married Women's Property Act of 1882 that married women were allowed to make wills in their own rights, although this Act must have been frowned on by the majority of husbands who had been used to owning their wives and their property from the dawn of time! Wills could be made by spinsters and widows, however.

If a will had not been made, an estate would often be settled quite amicably by the relatives concerned without Letters of Administration being applied for. If there was considerable property or if there was any dissension within the family then Letters of Administration would be applied for, from the appropriate court.

It must be remembered here that some wills were made a few years before death, and that probate, because of various disputes and litigations may have taken several years to complete, although this was more the exception than the rule; even so, it does pay to search several years after death for a will.

An example is shown in the abstract of the will of Roger Molford of Burrington in Devon who dictated his will on 25 February 1640 when, as it was stated, 'he was sick and weak in body'. Within three weeks he had died and was buried on 20 March 1640. Because of various court actions and disputes his will was not proved until 32 years later with his only surviving daughter acting as executrix, his wife Zenobia and other daughter Grace having died in the intervening years.

Abstract of the will of Roger Molford

MOLFORD, Roger of Brudge in Burrington, Gent., . . . sick and weak in body:

Will dated 25th February 1640.

Proved 7th June 1672 by Amy Rosier *alias* Molford, surviving executrix. On oath taken 9th May 1672 before Christopher Baitson.

To the poor of Burrington 30/-
To my wife Zenobia all my furniture (except that standing in the Broad Chamber at Northam in such sort as it was given by my father to my daughter Grace and one other bedstead given to my daughter Amy) and after her death to my daughters Grace and Amy equally.

To Christopher Baitson of Chulmleigh Clerk and John Challacomb of Westleigh, John Davy *als* Richards of Yeaberley and George Risdon of Parkham, gents and their heirs all my lands etc., in Northam, Burrington, Abbotsham, Winckleigh, Tawton Episcopi and elsewhere, also my Rectory of Burrington and the Vicarage of the said parish to go also with the Sheaf, Garb and Tithes and the nomination, donation etc., of the said Vicarage, upon trust to satisfy my debts and legacies and subject thereto to my daughters Grace and Amy and their heirs. The remainder to Edward Reed, the younger, son of Edward Reed the elder of Trayne gent; Thomas Challacombe, son of John Challacombe of Westleigh, gent and George Risdon the younger son of George Risdon the elder of Parkham, gent and their heirs.
Residue to my two daughters whom I make my executors.

Signed: Roger Molford

Witnesses: Anne Wood
John Bright

Proved Exeter, Barum Archdeaconry.

The Prerogative Court of Canterbury or the PCC

The Prerogative Court of Canterbury (The Archbishop of Canterbury's Court) also known as the *PCC* covered all counties in the south of the country with wills and administrations dating from 1383 to 1858. This court, the highest in the land, was the probate court for the rich and upper class families who owned property all over the country, although there was nothing to stop any executor travelling to London to have a will proved if he wished.

Non-conformists who wished to refrain from any dealings with the established church, seamen, soldiers, anyone who had died abroad and who had property in this country, or a person living in this country with property overseas, would have their wills proved in this court. It is essential that PCC will and administrations should always be closely looked at by the genealogist.

From 1653 to 1660 the time of the Commonwealth, all wills and administrations were proved in the Prerogative Court of Canterbury as they came under the jurisdiction of the State.

During these seven years, probate and administration was given to judges appointed by Parliament and jurisdiction by the church courts was abolished, therefore all wills and administrations during these years are to be found in the PCC almost without exception.

Death Duty Registers or Inland Revenue Wills

The Legacy Duty Act of 1796 made a duty payable on legacies and residues of the personal estate of a deceased person. These duties were payable on certain types of bequests and groups defined by their degree of kinship to the deceased. This duty was extended by the Legacy Duty Act of 1805 and the Stamp Act of 1815 to money legacies and residues bequeathed in wills which were to be raised by the sale of real estate.

The Death Duty registers extend from 1796 to 1894, but from 1858 these wills will be found in the records of the Principal Probate Registry wills and administrations in Somerset House; even so, it is still advisable to search the Death Duty registers from 1858 to 1894 as well.

These registers are a finding aid to the court in which the will or administration was granted, and by using these indexes and the registers together to identify the entry for the deceased, it is then possible to find the Will which should be deposited in the appropriate county record office, or in the Public Record Office if proved in the Prerogative Court of Canterbury.

During the Second World War, most of the wills for Devon, Somerset, and part of Cornwall, which were in the probate registry at Exeter, were destroyed by the bombing but copies of wills from the Estate Duty office from 1812 to 1857, are now to be found in the respective record offices of these three counties.

Inventories

In general, an inventory may exist up to 1782, although, as is always the way, there are exceptions to this date with some existing beyond 1782. An inventory is of the personal estate of a deceased's goods and chattles — furniture, clothes, money, crops and debts owed and owing. Generally, the only reference to land will be found in the mention of leases and mortgages.

Where Letters of Administration were taken out for intestate persons, an inventory was nearly always taken. Up to 1782 every executor or administrator was obliged to return an inventory of the deceased's belongings, but having said this, it is a matter of 'survival rate' as to whether an inventory is still in existence, but a search should always be made for one.

An inventory can give a striking picture of the layout of an ancestor's home as it lists each room together with the value of all items found in it.

Where to find Wills, Letters of Administration and Inventories

Generally, wills, administrations and inventories for the minor courts such as those of the Archdeacon, Bishop, Dean, or a Peculiar are to be found in county record offices or other local repositories. Prerogative Court of Canterbury wills and administrations and the Estate Duty wills and administrations register are at the Public Record Office, Chancery Lane, London WC2A 1LR. There are lists of indexes to these on shelves in the Rolls Room, in year order then in alphabetical order but not in any specific order within the letter of the alphabet. Inventories which accompany wills and administrations of the PCC are also to be found in this room. A reader's ticket is needed for the Public Record Office (see Chapter 13).

The Prerogative Court of York wills and administrations are at the Borthwick Institute, University of York, St. Anthony's Hall, York, YO1 2PW.

Welsh wills are at the National Library of Wales, Aberystwyth, Wales, except for PCC wills which are at Chancery Lane.

Inventory of the goods and chattles of Oliver Nickliss of Keyston, Huntingdonshire dated 1769

Most Scottish wills before and after the year 1823 are at the Scottish Record Office, General Register House, Edinburgh, EH1 3YY, but some may still be found with the Sheriffs' courts.

Irish wills which survived the 1922 troubles, when the Four Courts was destroyed, are at the Public Record Office of Ireland, Four Courts, Dublin, Ireland. For Northern Ireland, they are at the Public Record Office of Northern Ireland, Belfast, N. Ireland. There are lists and indexes to all wills at both of these record offices.

Occasionally, the word *Inhibition* crops up with regards to probate of wills, meaning that the Bishop periodically 'visited' his clergy, that is to say that they were summoned to appear before him and during this 'visitation' all the lower courts were inhibited or closed during this time for a period of a few months, and only the Bishops Court would prove a will at this time.

A Bishopric would become vacant whilst waiting for a new Bishop to be appointed, and wills and administrations would not then be proved in the Bishop's Court but another court, usually that of the Dean and Chapter, or the Prerogative Court of Canterbury would take over probate.

Comments

- A bishop's diocese is not a county. In some cases a Bishop's Diocese may encompass part of a county or more than one county. Every area of England and Wales is covered by a bishop's diocese.
- If a deceased had debts in more than one jurisdiction then the same process as described for property in more than one jurisdiction applied.
- It must be remembered that — as with all ancient documents — wills, administrations, and inventories may not have survived the ravages of time and man.
- Often children were provided for in a marriage settlement and therefore may not be mentioned in a will.
- 'Cut off with a shilling' — unless this is definitely stated in a will, a token shilling may be left to a daughter (usually married) who had already received her portion or dowry on marriage, or a son who had received money for an apprenticeship or business, or possibly on his marriage.
- Some very early wills were not signed by the testator.
- Take note of witnesses and executors of a will as they may be 'family'.
- A Holograph will was one written in the the deceased's own handwriting and did not need witnesses, only affirmation from two or three people who knew him, stating that the will was in the deceased's own handwriting.
- Transcribe a will or administration exactly as it has been written and make a 'family tree' from the information given and pin it to your copy. This will give you 'at a glance' information which may tie-in with your research into other records.
- County maps showing will jurisdictions in different colours are an invaluable aid to research.
- Death Duty Registers contain abstracts of wills only.
- By the Married Women's Property Act Of 1882/83, a wife was for the first time, able to buy, own, sell property, and to keep her wages without the consent of her husband.

An example of how wills were proved in the ecclesiastical courts before 1858

Probate Jurisdictions

The Archdeacon's Court would have jurisdiction and would normally prove wills or grant letters of administration if the testator's (deceased's) property fell within the area of the archdeaconry.

For example, if a Henry Jones, deceased, had held property only in the town of Swindon, Wiltshire, then as Swindon came under the jurisdiction of the Archdeacon of Wiltshire, his will would have been proved in the Archdeacon of Wiltshire's court.

The Bishop's Diocesan Court, known as the *Consistory Court* or the *Commissary Court* (part of a Bishop's Court) had jurisdiction if the property was held in more than one Archdeaconry.

For example, taking once more our mythical Henry Jones, deceased, if he had property in Swindon, Wiltshire, the Archdeacon of Wiltshire's jurisdiction and also property in Amesbury, Wiltshire, which came under the jurisdiction of the Archdeacon of Salisbury, then his will would have been proved in the Bishop of Salisbury's Consistory Court and not in either of the two Archdeacons' courts at all (see also, 'Inhibition' on page 86).

If the deceased's property was held in more than one diocese then his will would have been proved in the *Archbishop's Courts* of which there were two called *Provinces* — *The Prerogative Court of Canterbury* and *The Prerogative Court of York*. If, however, the deceased's property fell into more than one province, the *Prerogative Court of Canterbury* as the senior province in the land would prove the will.

To carry on the example of Henry Jones' will further — if Henry Jones, deceased, had been a reasonably wealthy man and had owned property in more than one diocese, such as the Bishop of Salisbury's diocese, and also that of the Bishop of Exeter, then his will would *not* be proved in either of these two Bishops' Consistory courts but would have been proved in the appropriate Archbishop's Court — in this case, that of the Archbishop of Canterbury or the Prerogative Court of Canterbury.

If, however, our Henry Jones, deceased, had been an extremely wealthy man and had happened to own property, for example, in both Wiltshire and Lancashire, his will would have then been proved in the Archbishop of Canterbury's Court as the senior court in the land.

On first reading, this business of proving wills seems to be very complicated, but when your research takes you into the realms of will hunting, you will soon become familiar with the procedure and find it is nowhere so involved as it seemed initially.

Wills after 1858

The subject of wills from the time the civil authorities became involved, is not nearly so complicated as before 11 January 1858. Since that date, all wills and administrations for England and Wales have been proved in the Principal Probate Registry, London or in the District Probate Registries. The indexes to these wills have been bound, one volume per year, and are available for free public scrutiny at Somerset House, London. Each volume is comprised of separate books, the number depending on how many wills were proved in that year. All are in alphabetical order and are extremely simple and straight-forward to use.

Although the indexes are free to view, fees have to be paid to see a copy of a will; such copies can be ordered to read, or copy extracts from, within a few minutes. Should you want a photocopy of the document for your files, then a small fee is paid on the spot and the copy is sent to your address, usually within a few days. These may also be ordered by post. A list of current charges may be obtained by sending an S.A.E. to the Principal Registry of the Family Division, Somerset House, The Strand, London, WC2R 1LP. The office is open from Monday to Friday 10 a.m. to 4.30 p.m. One word of warning must be given when searching for a will. It may have taken some time for it to have been proved after the person died, so don't expect to find an entry on the same week as the death took place.

If a person died without making a will (intestate), letters of administration, often known as 'admons', could have been issued.

Up to the year 1870, although wills and admons appear in the same volumes, they are separate, with wills in the first half of the book and admons in the last half. After this date, wills and administrations are combined in the indexes.

The entries in the indexes usually give a brief account of the details, such as name and address, date and place of death, and often occupation of the deceased, executors and the total amount of the effects, but it is always worthwhile seeing a copy of the will.

Abbreviations used in Wills

Admon	Letters of Administration
Bd	Bond — a signed and witnessed obligation
Cod	Codicil — an addition to a will
Exec	Executor/Executrix
Inv	Inventory
IR	Inland Revenue
PCC	Prerogative Court of Canterbury
PCY	Prerogative Court of York
PPR	Principal Probate Registry, Somerset House
Prob	Probate
Wpr	Will proved

Here follows a list of the District Probate Registries and the dates of local indexes held. Also included are dates from which certain County Record Offices hold indexes for the area. For this list we are indebted to Eve McLaughlin, it appears in her book, *Somerset House Wills*, published by the Federation of Family History Societies.

Avon: Bristol (indexes from 1901).
Indexes (1858-1900): Bristol Record Office.

Cambs: Peterborough.
Indexes: Cambridgeshire Record Office, Huntingdon branch.
Cheshire: Chester. Indexes: Cheshire Record Office.
Cornwall: Bodmin (also indexes).
Cumbria: Carlisle.
Indexes: Cumbria Record Office, Carlisle branch.
Devon: Exeter (also indexes).
Glos: Gloucester.
Indexes: Gloucestershire Record Office (daily charge, £1).
Greater Manchester: Manchester.
Indexes: Greater Manchester County RO (notice required).
Hampshire: Winchester.
Indexes: Hampshire Record Office.
Humberside: Hull.
Kent: Maidstone.
Lancs: Lancaster.
Indexes: Lancashire Record Office, Preston.
Leics: Leicester (indexes from 1887).
Indexes, 1858-1886: Leicestershire RO (notice required).
Lincs: Lincoln.
Indexes: Lincolnshire Archives Office.
Merseyside: Liverpool.
Indexes: Liverpool Record Office.
Norfolk: Norwich (also indexes).
Northants: See Cambs.
Northumberland: see Tyne and Wear.
Notts: Nottingham.
Indexes: Nottinghamshire Record Office.
Oxon: Oxford.
Indexes: Bodleian Library (Radcliffe Camera) (£1 daily charge).
Staffs: Stoke on Trent.
Suffolk: Ipswich (no indexes held locally).
East Sussex: Brighton.
Indexes: East Sussex Record Office, Lewes.
Tyne and Wear: Newcastle-upon-Tyne (also indexes).
West Midlands: Birmingham.
Indexes: Birmingham Reference Library.
North Yorks: Middlesbrough.
York (also Indexes).
South Yorks: Sheffield.
Indexes: South Yorkshire RO.
West Yorks: Leeds.
Indexes: West Yorkshire County Record Office, Wakefield.

Dyfed: Carmarthen.
    Indexes: National Library of Wales, Aberystwyth.
        Dyfed Archives, Carmarthen Branch Office.
Glamorgan: Llandaff.
    Indexes: Glamorgan Archive Service, Cardiff.
Gwynedd: Bangor.
    Indexes: Gwynedd Archives Service, Caernarfon Area RO.

For addresses of District Probate Registries, Record Offices and telephone numbers see *Record Offices: How to find them* by J.S.W. Gibson and P. Peskett (FFHS).

Scotland

A leaflet giving details of the holdings of wills in Edinburgh may be obtained by sending a large stamped addressed envelope to The Scottish Record Office, HM General Register House, Edinburgh.

Principal Probate Registry Will

The Last Will and Testament of Samuel Elstone, yeoman, of Higher Way, Tiverton, Devon dated 4th July 1862.

In the name of God Amen. The Last Will of Samuel Elstone Yeoman of Higher Way Farm in the parish of Tiverton in the county of Devon in perfect body and mind and knowing it is appointed unto men once to die And as touching such worldly Estate and Goods wherewith it hath pleased God to bless me with in this life I give and despose of the same in the following manner and form and first I give and bequeath unto my daughter Elizabeth the wife of Edmund Bond the sum of One Shilling. I also give bequeath unto my daughter Emma the wife of Danial Trude One Shilling. I give and bequeath unto my wife Elizabeth and nine of my children namely William, Samuel, Henry, Edwin, John, Mary Ann, Selina, Caroline Jane, Frederic all my Goods and Chattles money and securities for money credits and effects of what nature or kind whatsoever. But in case my wife should marry again and after the second marriage takes place, in that event, to leave the business and property to my nine children. But if either of the children should get married or wish to leave after they arrive at the age of twenty one years of age then for my two Trustees namely William Blake, Yeoman, Templeton and William Elstone, Yeoman, Witheridge both in the County of Devon to decide what share of the property they shall have, after all debts and expenses is paid. And lastly I charge my Goods and Chattles to the payments of all my just debts funeral and testamentary expenses to my wife Elizabeth and nine of my children as before mentioned joint Executrix and Executors of this my last will and Testament made by me.

In Witness whereof I have hereunto subscribed my name this fourth of July in the year of our Lord, One thousand, eight hundred and sixty two...........

.... Samuel Elston .... Signed, published and declared by me Samuel Elstone the Testator as and for my last will and testament in the presence of us who have subscribed our names at witness thereunto in the presence and at the request of the Testator and in the presence of each other .... William Blake .... Nutcombe Cornwall ....

On the 13th day of February 1863 the will of Samuel Elston late of Tiverton in the County of Devon Farmer deceased was proved by the Oath of Elizabeth Elston, widow, the Relict of the deceased, one of the Executors she having been first sworne duly to administer, power being reserved to Mary Ann Elston, spinster, William Elston, Samuel Elston, Henry Elston, children of the deceased and to Edwin Elston, Selina Elston, spinster, John Elston, Caroline Jane Elston, spinster and Frederick in the will written Frederic Elston, minors. Children of the deceased the other Executors when they shall attain the sum of twenty one years.

Effects under £600.

Extracted by R.G. Tucker, Solicitor, Tiverton

I certify that the above is a correct copy of the original will of Samuel Elston, deceased ....

Further reading

Wills and Where to Find Them by J.S.W. Gibson (Phillimore 1974).
Wills and Their Whereabouts by Anthony Camp (Society of Genealogists).
A Simplified Guide to Probate Jurisdictions — Where to look for wills compiled by J.S.W. Gibson. (Gulliver Press and FFHS).
Wills before 1858 by Eve McLaughlin (McLaughlin Guide, FFHS).
Somerset House Wills by Eve McLaughlin (McLaughlin Guide, FFHS).
Goods and Chattles of our Forefathers ed. by J.S. Moore (Phillimore 1976).
Tracing Your Ancestors in the Public Record Office by Jane Cox and Timothy Padfield (HMSO).
A Glossary of Household, Farming and Trade Terms from Probate Inventories by Rosemary Milward (Derbyshire Record Society 1982).
Parish maps for each county, showing probate jurisdictions from the Institute of Heraldic and Genealogical Studies, Northgate, Canterbury, Kent.

CHAPTER 7

Parish Records, Civil Records, Poor Law, Quarter Session Records and Records of the Clerk of the Peace

Introduction

These are the records, which, in genealogist's terms, 'put the flesh on the bare bones' of a family history. They are generally to be found in the possession of the county record office or the relevant authorites (see Chapter 8).

After having tracked down your ancestors by using the step-by-step guide given in previous chapters in this book and having drawn up a family tree with names, dates and places already discovered, the time has now come to seek further information from the records, not only to confirm that your research is correct, but to find out just what happened to your ancestors during their lifetimes. In this way you will travel back in time through the fortunes, or misfortunes of the family, discovering more about them and their way of life.

This can be one of the most fascinating aspects of family history which enables you, the family historian, to find out more about the ordinary and at times, the not so ordinary, men and women who are your ancestors.

You will find that all families had their 'ups and downs' throughout the generations who may range from some of the highest born in the land to the lowliest of labourers toiling in the fields to scratch a living. You may discover teachers, lawyers, clergymen, yeomen, land-owners and magistrates or tradesmen, craftsmen, servants and agricultural labourers, and so on.

It will be more than likely that some members of the family may have been incapable of working through ill-health or a handicap of some kind, often caused by a poor diet and overwork and bad living conditions — disorders, which in today's world would be treatable and curable, but which, in the 'good old days' were not. Many of our ancestors fell foul of the law and were harshly dealt with by the justices and courts for what we would now consider relatively minor misdemeanours. These offences were very often committed because of their poor circumstances purely in order to feed and clothe their families. Of course, some broke the law for the sheer joy of it. Illegitimate children appear with startling regularity from generation to generation in families.

Bearing all these facts in mind, whenever a family has been established in a certain place for at least one generation, then the documents and records of that place should be examined for evidence of the family and their background for that particular period of time.

Many of the documents found in parish, civil and records of the clerk of the peace are very closely related to one another, and, of necessity, have been put together into one chapter under their various headings. Just as a parish has its officials together with their various papers and books, so does a civil authority. Overlying all these are the Quarter Session records and those of the Clerk of the Peace, for the justices or magistrates worked closely with the ecclesiastical and civil officials. Therefore, the same types of papers will be found in all these records and they must be searched to put the family into the context of the times in which they lived.

Parish records

Following the 1538 mandate by Thomas Cromwell, Henry VIII's chief minister, a 'sure coffer' made of sturdy oak was required to be kept in the church to store all the parish books, records, registers, and documents relating to parish business. The coffer known as the 'Parish Chest' also contained all the parish silver and communion plate.

This requirement led to the survival of many of the parish records available to family historians today, and they are the ones which concerned the everyday lives of our ancestors from the time they were born, married, died and were buried.

The minister of the parish church such as a rector, vicar, or curate would be instituted to the living, often by the lord of the manor or some other person who held the 'gift of the living', and it was he, the minister, who saw to the moral and spiritual welfare of his parishioners. Local magistrates, who were of the gentry, not only saw to the welfare of their tenants but administered the law and meted out punishment where necessary. They, like the minister and his parish officials, formed an integral part of the parish community.

Each year, a parish council comprised of responsible citizens, and some rate-paying householders, known as the Vestry, administered parish affairs and elected officers to carry out their various duties in the parish, all unpaid, except for the incumbent and the parish clerk.

The Vestry

The Vestry, the parish council, was composed of reliable inhabitants and ones who were capable of organizing and governing the parish. The meeting was usually chaired, traditionally by the parish minister. This parochial parliament developed about the fifteenth century and as a body, discussed and voted on church business, later on acquiring other powers of decision and supervision in the parish. They worked in conjunction with the justices of the peace.

There were two kinds of vestry meetings, the 'closed' or 'select' and the 'open'. The closed or select vestry was the governing body of the parish generally having property qualifications. The open vestry was a general meeting held periodically for all inhabitants of rate-paying households.

Vestry minutes can be one of the most revealing of books, bearing in mind the power that this august body of men held within their grasp as they levied fines, audited the parish officers' accounts, and if necessary, made arrangements and payments for the emigration of parish paupers to the colonies.

It is interesting to note in one parish deep in the heart of rural Wessex that the vestry members used to open their meetings in the church vestry, promptly adjourn only to re-open in the local hostelry where there was warmth and comfort. The vestry accounts for this particular parish always included a substantial sum for bread, cheese and ale — all on the rates!

Churchwardens

Two, or maybe more churchwardens for a large parish, were appointed and sworn into their office on Easter Tuesday each year. One was the Vicar's warden and the other the People's warden. This office was an ancient one dating back to the twelfth century. The churchwardens' duties were many and at times could be interchangeable with the Overseers of the Poor and the Constable. They were responsible for the guardianship and upkeep of the church fabric and property. They also reported to the appropriate ecclesiastical court such as the Archdeacon or Bishop on the morals and welfare of the parishioners, including the minister, 'presenting' twice a year whether anything was amiss or irregular in the parish.

Churchwardens' account books and vouchers are very comprehensive in that villagers and tradesmen are named in them for supplies and maintenance and cleaning of the church and grounds. These accounts usually include the fee to the parish clerk for the keeping of the registers, as well as the administration of charities (see Chapter 12), extinction of vermin, allocation of pews and their rents and the purchase of sacramental wine and bread.

Churchwardens' Vouchers, Brampton, Huntingdonshire — purchase of a cottage dated 1774

The Disbursements of M[r] John Walker & Peter Lamb Churchwardens from Easter 1791 to Easter 1792

Peter Lambs Disbursements	£	S	D
Paid for Sparrows at various Times	1	1	5½
Paid Baxter for Mend[g] Church Wall	0	2	0
July 21th Paid Ric[d] Corthorn for Matts for the Church	0	2	6
Paid for Hedge Hogs various Times	0	2	4
Sep. 22[d] Paid the Ringers at W[m] Hills	0	5	0
Paid at the visitation	0	7	0
Oct[r] 7th Paid the Presentment Bill	0	7	0
D[o] 12th Paid Geo Chambers Qut[r] Bill	1	3	3
D[o] 31th Paid for Hedghogs	0	1	2
Nov 5th Paid the Ringers at W[m] Lowthers	0	5	0
D[o] 12th Paid for a Hedghog	0	0	4
Paid for a Bill Rope	0	4	0
Paid Presentment Bill & Exp	0	9	6
Paid Geo Clarks Bill	0	5	6
Nov 20th Paid Wollarson for Mend[g] Church Wall	0	2	0
Paid for two Hedghogs	0 .	0	8
Paid for two Broomes for Street	0	0	6
Dec 19th Paid M[r] Head for Visitation Expen	0	15	0
Jan 10th Paid for Broomes for the Street	0	2	0
1792 Paid for a Hedghog Feb 27th	0	0	4
Mar 29th Paid W[m] Chambers Paving Bill	5	5	4
	£ 11	2	6¼

Churchwardens' Accounts dated 1791-1792 for Yaxley, Huntingdon-shire

Overseers of the poor

This particular office was created by an act in 1572 followed by another in

1597/8 which ordered the appointment of overseers by the justices. In 1601 came the Poor Law Act, made permanent in 1640 which was the basis of poor law administration throughout the country for nearly two hundred years until 1834. The Poor Law Acts provided for the making of churchwardens as overseers of the poor and the duties of these responsible householders and

Overseers of the Poor Account Book for Morchard Bishop, Devon dated 1763

pillars of the community were onerous in that they maintained the able-bodied poor and set them to work; relieved the sick and aged, known as the 'impotent poor'; apprenticed poor or pauper children; assisted the parish constable in his duties and set a rate to tax every inhabitant and occupier of land to pay for the upkeep of the poor. They also provided a House of Correction for vagrants as well as a Poor House.

Brampton Poor Account Book 1807

Overseers of the Poor account books and vouchers show rates and rate-payers' names and payments of every kind to the poor who are named, in the way of clothing and food, with some poor being maintained by the poor rate from the cradle to the grave. The accounts are very detailed, giving over a period of years a social study of a village and its inhabitants.

Parish constable (petty constable)

The post of parish constable was one of the most ancient posts and was important in that he had to maintain law and order in the parish community. He was supervised in his duties by the churchwardens and the justices of the peace. It was not a popular job and there was a widespread practice of paying someone else to do the work. This post was eventually superseded by the Parish Constables Act of 1842, and from this time on parish constables were appointed at special sessions of the justices, the post surviving until about 1862.

From 1842 records of their appointments will be found in the records of the Clerk of the Peace. From 1757 parish men were chosen by ballot to serve for three years in the militia or, if they had enough money, they could pay for a substitute. Part of the constable's function was to see that this procedure ran smoothly. The parish constable had powers of arrest and could take in charge anyone who had committed a crime or a breach of the peace and he was able to hold that person in custody in the stocks, the local lock-up or cage, or in his own home until such time as the prisoner was brought before the magistrates. If sentence was passed the constable would deliver the prisoner to gaol. As well as parish constables there were also the high constables of the hundreds and headboroughs or tithingmen of townships, all unpaid for their duties.

Constables' accounts and vouchers may be found in the collection in the parish chest and some expenses may also appear in the overseers' and churchwardens' accounts. Militia papers, discharges and payments to families may be found in the parish chest documents or in the records of the Clerk of the Peace.

Surveyors of the highways (overseers of the highways/waywarden/stonewarden)

The 1555 Highway Act gave responsibility for the upkeep of the highway to parishes and provided for one or two surveyors to be appointed for each parish to ensure that all roads and bridges within the parish were maintained. All able-bodied parishioners were required to give so many days labour on the roads. Able-bodied poor were also set to work picking stones from the fields for the roads. This post was another unpaid appointment which was unpopular. By 1691 power of appointment of the surveyors was transferred from the parish to the justices.

Documents concerning the surveyors of the highways are Highways accounts and vouchers although there may be mention in overseers' and churchwardens' accounts as well.

Constables' Accounts for Brampton, Huntingdonshire dated 1718

Rector, vicar, curate

As well as parish registers, bishops' transcripts, and other diocesan papers for which the minister of a parish was responsible, the survey known as a *Glebe Terrier* and *Tithe documents* belong with the papers of the parish incumbent.

Diocesan (Archdeaconry of Huntingdon) 'Glebe Terrier' — no date Alwalton, Huntingdon.

A Glebe Terrier was a survey of land and an inventory of the glebes, lands, fields, houses and tithes of land which were part of his benefice. These terriers generally commence about the sixteenth and seventeenth centuries and are important in that they may give ancestral names and occupations for all those people who owned or leased land which bordered upon the glebe lands. Glebe Terriers may also be found in Diocesan Records (see Chapter 8).

Tithe records — a rector or vicar of a parish was entitled to a tenth part of the main produce of the land, such as grain crops, and wood and this was known as a *Praedial Tithe* (arising from the produce of the land), plus the tenth part of the produce of stock and labour such as milk, wool, pigs, known as a *Mixed Tithe* (coming from the stock on the land), and *Personal Tithe* (from the labour of the occupiers of the land). All these tithes were paid by parishioners to the church. Tithes were then divided into *Great* or *Rectorial Tithes* (for a Rector) and *Small or Vicarial Tithes* (for a Vicar). Gradually, this system became outdated and very unwieldy and eventually by the Tithe Commutation Act of 1836 all tithes were converted into cash payments by commissioners, a much more satisfactory form of payment. The result was the *Tithe Awards* which were arranged alphabetically under landowners with occupiers, acreage and the annual tithe payment. There is also shown on the Award a number which refers to the parish *Tithe map* which shows houses, field names, land and boundaries. This map and the award can, therefore, easily be cross-referenced to find exactly where an ancestor lived within a parish.

Tithe awards and maps may also be found in county record offices or at the Public Record Office at Kew, Richmond, Surrey.

Civil records

As stated in the introduction to this chapter, civil records are those of a large village, town, city, borough and county. These are closely allied with those of the ecclesiastical parishes and officers within their boundaries and, as such, their records will be of a similar nature to those of a parish. Just as the parish records are tied up with those of the justices of the peace, so are the civil ones.

For example: the ancient town of Marlborough in Wiltshire had two parish churches, St. Mary's and St. Peter and St. Paul, and was an important town in olden days. It had a mayor and council, a gaol or bridewell and workhouse. Not only are there all the records of the two parishes but also the ones of the town, some of them being the same type as found in the parish. Other documents relate to inhabitants such as rate books, council minutes, town apprentices, burgess rolls, rents, charities, and so on.

If ancestry is found in such a place as this then all civil records should be carefully searched as well as those of the parish. County Councils were set up under the Local Government Act of 1888 to replace the Courts of Quarter Sessions in most of their administrative functions but although local government records may not necessarily be so valuable as those of the parish and civil documents they can still be of help for more in-depth work on certain subjects.

Other documents which may have survived and appear either in the parish chest collection or in civil records are such items as minister's visiting books,

Brampton Apprentice Indenture Mary Hodd to John Tompson, Victualler of Brampton — 13 Sept 1709

local charities (see Chapter 12), confirmation lists, Sunday school registers, and other school admission records.

Lastly, special mention must be made of apprentices and apprenticeship indentures, a most important source for the genealogist. An apprenticeship was the system of training for all skilled trades. It was maintained by guilds from about 1350 without any statutory sanction but when the power of the guilds started to decline the apprenticeship system received definite statutory sanction by the passing of the Statute of Apprentices in 1562. The Statute stated that a uniform term of seven years' apprenticeship should be served as a condition of the right to practise any manual trade and this was quite rigidly enforced until well into the eighteenth century. By 1710 some apprenticeships were taxed, duty was liable on all indentures at the rate of 6d in the pound on premiums of £50 and under, and 1s in the pound on sums over £50. In fact, this tax remained in force for a century. From 1710 to around 1760 much valuable information is given in these registers, as not only is the apprentice's name given along with his or her master or mistress, but parishes, trades and dates as well. From these registers which are to be found in the Public Record Office under the grouping of the Inland Revenue (I.R.) one can see where an ancestor may have come from to serve an apprenticeship and where he or she may have stayed on completion of their term, perhaps to settle down and marry.

Pauper children, however, were treated quite differently from premium paying apprentices as they were forcibly apprenticed, quite often against the will of their parents, for a small amount of money from a master or mistress payable to the parish, for much longer than the term of seven years, thus relieving the parish of a burden. Poor children were often apprenticed from the age of 7 years old to 21 years for girls and 24 years for boys until 1768 when the age was reduced to 21 years for boys.

These apprenticeships supposedly had two useful aspects, one being that the child was learning a useful trade although very often the child was used as a household menial who belonged to their master or mistress until their term of service was up, the other aspect was that the churchwardens and overseers were ridding themselves of a charge on the poor rate, with the employer gaining cheap labour for the sum of £5, or so. If a boy, while apprenticed, should, by some unfortunate chance, be 'impressed' into the navy, his master was entitled to all his pay and his prize money! Another type of apprenticeship was the charity apprenticeship, usually bestowed by some benevolent member of a parish in their will for the good of the poor children of the parish. This kind of apprenticeship had terms set down by which the parish officials, the master or mistress, and the apprentice had rights and conditions which ensured reasonably fair treatment.

Pauper apprenticeships and charity apprenticeship indentures and information will be found in the parish records and at times, in churchwardens accounts or the accounts of the overseers. Paid apprenticeships will also be found in the parish collection, and those where tax was paid to the government, from 1710 to around 1810, are to be found in the apprentice registers

Examinations concerning the Settlements of Thomas Bell and Elizabeth Butler dated 1850 Brampton, Huntingdonshire

in the Public Record Office, Chancery Lane, London. It is advisable to search these registers to find the whereabouts of a 'missing' forbear.

Settlement, examination and removal certificates

In 1662, a very important act was brought in, known as the Act of Settlement. This stated that a stranger staying in a parish could be removed by the over-seers within forty days if he had no means of being able to work, or if he did not rent property worth £10 a year. After forty days a stranger could claim that he was settled in the parish and therefore, if need arose he could claim settlement there, thus maybe becoming a charge on the poor rate. This act also authorized the justices to punish persistent vagrants.

Thirty-five years later in 1697 another Act of Settlement was passed which stated that strangers were allowed to enter a parish provided they possessed a settlement certificate showing they would be taken back by their home parish if they became in need of poor relief. If a stranger came into a parish for tem-porary work, for example, he was obliged to bring a certificate from his home parish guaranteeing to take him back.

The administration of these laws often caused confusion amongst magis-trates but the law itself was quite clear, that parish officials did not relieve a pauper, that is to say, give him poor relief unless he was in his own parish of settlement and it must be stressed that a 'parish of settlement' was not neces-sarily a parish of birth.

A person was able to gain settlement in a parish in several ways as follows:

By being born there if illegitimate.

By working there for at least one year if unmarried.

By serving a full apprenticeship in a parish.

By a woman marrying a husband there.

By having a father there if a child was legitimate and under 7 years of age.

By holding a public office.

By paying rates or by having 40 days' residence there after giving due notice in writing.

Churchwardens and Overseers of the Poor of the Parish of *Wimbledon* —
———— in the County of *Surrey* — and to each and every of them.

Huntingdonshire **WHEREAS** Complaint hath been made unto Us, whose Names are
to wit. hereunto set, and Seals affixed, being two of his Majesty's Justices
of the Peace in and for the County of HUNTINGDON aforesaid, (one whereof
being of the Quorum) by the Churchwardens and Overseers of the Poor of
the said Parish of *Godmanchester* ————
THAT

William Wright, and Alice his

wife

have come to, and do now inhabit in, the said Parish of *Godmanchester*,
not having gained a legal settlement there; and
that the said *William Wright and Ann*
his wife — are actually
~~are become~~ chargeable to the said Parish of *Godmanchester*
WE, the said Justices, upon due proof made thereof as well upon the

examination of the said *William Wright* ————

upon Oath, as other circumstances, and likewise upon due consideration
had of the premises, DO ADJUDGE the same to be true; and, do also
adjudge the place of the Legal Settlement of the said *William*
Wright and Ann his wife
to be in the Parish of *Wimbledon* ————
in the County of *Surrey* ————

THESE are therefore, in his Majesty's Name, to require you, the said
Churchwardens and Overseers of the Poor of the said Parish of *Godmanchester* — or some or one of you, on sight hereof, to remove and
convey the said *William Wright and*
Ann his wife
from and out of your said Parish of *Godmanchester*
to the said Parish of *Wimbledon* and them
deliver to the Churchwardens and Overseers of the Poor there, to some
or one of them, together with this our Order, or a true copy thereof
(at the same time shewing to them the Original). And we do also require
you, the said Churchwardens and Overseers of the Poor of the said Parish
of *Wimbledon* — to receive and provide for them
as Inhabitants of your Parish.

GIVEN under our Hands and Seals, at HUNTINGDON, the *Fourth*
———— day of *December*, in the Year of
our Lord, one thousand, eight hundred, and ~~twenty~~ *thirty*.

Jms Reynolds   *J Weston*

Removal certificate from Godmanchester, Huntingdonshire to Wimbledon, Surrey for William and Alice Wright dated 1830

upon that parish, then it became necessary to 'examine' the person if he or
she was not in possession of a settlement certificate.

From this detailed 'examination' by the justices it would be determined which
parish was the correct parish of settlement and the person or persons would
then either be issued with a settlement certificate for that parish or would

be 'removed' back to his or her own home parish, occasionally with a pass showing the route to be taken.

These vital and important settlement, examination, and removal certificates give evidence which can prove, for the family historian, just how, why and where a family may have disappeared to for a short space of time or where they may have moved to permanently. It is important to realize that some-

Godmanchester Settlement Certificate 1758. John Rose, miller. Catherine & Thomas, son of said John Rose by a former wife and John & Hannah Rose, children of said John Rose & Catherine his wife

Settlement Certificate to Brampton, Huntingdonshire, from Baldock, Hertfordshire, for Elizabeth Fox, dated 1822

times our forbears, being only human and, at times, crafty and devious, would conveniently 'lose' their certificate of settlement when travelling around the countryside with no money, seeking work, eventually resulting in an examination of their circumstances, origins and family details with a removal back 'to their parish'.

Removals could often lead to a person or family being removed to a parish sometimes miles away across country, to a parish which they had never known or only known briefly as a very young child. The law of settlement was not really altered until the passing of the 1876 Poor Law Amendment Act.

Examination of Wm. Johnson by the Justices in 1737, Marlborough, Wiltshire

The Examination of William Johnson —
12 June, 1737

| Borough of Marlborough in Wilts | To wit. The examination of Wm Johnson, taken on Oath the 12th Day of June 1737 Before Thomas Beavan, Gentl. Mayor, and Wm Gough. Gentl. Two of his Maties Justices of the peace of the said Burrough, as followeth |

Saith. That he was born in the City of Limerick in the King-dom of Ireland. — That he is a Weaver and Woolcomber by Trade and that he work'd at his said trade a Year and a halfe with one Moses Vine of Kenta Street in the parish of St George's in the Borough of Southwark — then maried wth one Mary Bowles of Swansey in Wales, but a Servt. at that time at the Bell and Bare in the Burrough of Southwark aforesd. and went with his said wife to Bristoll to work and work'd there with one Charles Crawley without Castle Gate abt three months, and his said wife with him — He left his said wife and went back to London again and work'd for himselfe, till about Five or Six Weekes agoe (During wch time, he left his said wife behind him at Bristoll aforesaid) Then went to the Devizes and work'd there abt three Weekes wth one Mrs Pile — Then went to Bristoll to seek for his said wife. But when he came there, under-stood she was gone up to London after him. Five Weekes before, — Then was making his way up towards London again, and Tuesday last met her with two Men, abt four or five Miles beyond Bath — Ask'd her wt she had done wth the Child, and she told him she had left it at the Six Bells in Marlbrough, to wch place he saith he is now come for his said child

Saith. That he was maried to his said wife, abt Michas last, at the hand and penn in the Fleet, within the said City of London, and when he went away from her as aforesaid to London, he left her big wth Child and therefore suppos'd She had been brt to bed, when he so met her and ask'd her for there Child as before Set Forth ....

        Sworn before us the Day
        and Year aforesaid.
        Thos. Bevan   Wm. Johnson
        Wm. Gough

Rec'd of the Churchwardens and Overseers of St. Peter's Marlborough A Male Child Which was found att the Ring of Bells in sd. Parish last Sunday Morning. I own my self to be the true father of the Child and do promise the Parish to take due Care of the same as witness my hand this 12th day of June 1737.

        Witness
        Tho. Hodges   Wm. Johnson
        Anne Hodges

Wm. Johnson from ye Citty of Lymerick and Mary Bowls from Swansey being ye Fathr and Mothr of Thos. Johnson.

The vagrancy laws and vagrants

The vagrancy laws were much harsher than the settlement laws in that unscrupulous overseers could take advantage and would save on the expense of removing a stranger from their parish by not 'removing' him directly to his home parish, but they could, if they decided by an examination that he was a vagrant, pass him from one village boundary to another, from House of Correction to House of Correction until he arrived home. These costs would then be born by every parish through which he passed, thus saving the overseers the cost of a 'removal'.

Similarly, if a single woman or widow-woman of child-bearing years, or expecting a child, appeared suddenly within their midsts they would be rather anxious to rid themselves of this burden for, if she became pregnant, or had

Pass for Robert Little and his family to return to Broad Hinton in Wiltshire, issued by the Middlesex Magistrates in 1801

Vagrant Order for Elizabeth Sayer aged 12 years dated 1741, from Heylesbury, Wiltshire, to Wellford, Gloucestershire

the child in the parish then that child became 'settled' in that parish, although by 1743 children born illegitimately within a parish which was not the mother's place of settlement were then legally settled in their mother's home parish and not in the parish of their birth. If a father of an illegitimate child, especially if he was from another parish, could be persuaded to marry the mother, then the woman and her child would become settled in his parish.

An Act of 1743/4 put vagrants into three classifications 'idle and disorderly persons', 'rogues and vagabonds' and 'incorrigible rogues'. It is easy to see that there were many devious ways of ridding a parish of undesirable persons.

However, there were persistent vagrants, who, for one reason or another, tramped the countryside causing a nuisance, maybe because they had 'itchy feet' or because they were homeless, out of work, or were trying to escape the law. These were the people who were dealt with severely by the magistrates for consistently breaking the vagrancy laws. They were sentenced by whipping, sometimes branding, hard labour and sometimes, as a last resort, transportation to the colonies.

In the city of Salisbury there were vagrants from all over the kingdom as in the case of one Thomasin Ridgeway who on 21 February 1601 was described as an idle person and a vagrant accompanied by Robert Jones. She was punished by whipping and sent back to Dorset, where she was born, being given seven days to reach there, handed over from constable to constable along the way. Robert Jones, on examination, said that Thomasin was his wife but after her examination she confessed they were never married and had been together for half a year. Robert Jones was whipped and sent back to his home town of Canterbury in Kent.

In 1610, Mary Crosse, also known as Mary Wells wandering as a vagrant was spared punishment as she was 'great with child' and near her time — she was given six days to return to Somerset.

So, the authorities, although relieving the city from unwanted vagrants, did have some compassion towards pregnant women, the very young and the sick and elderly by sparing them the punishment of a public whipping.

Bastardy

It is a rare occurrence for family historians to discover no illegitimacy in their ancestry at all. An Act of 1575/6 decreed that mothers and fathers of a bastard child were to be punished and sent to prison by the magistrates. The Act of 1609 did not really improve matters concerning illegitimacy, as this stated that any lewd woman having a bastard chargeable may be sent to the House of Correction unless she gave security for good behaviour.

From the seventeenth century onwards until the middle of the eighteenth century, illegitimacy grew rapidly and another act in 1732/3 stated that a pregnant woman had to declare to the Overseers of the Poor that she was pregnant and to give the name of the father. Entries in parish registers at this time are to the effect 'reputed father .... as she saith' or, as shown in a baptism at Milton Lilbourne, Wiltshire, on 5 August 1787: John son, bastard of Ruth Tarrant — husband gone — and Guy Warwick.

The next Act of 1743/4 laid down that a bastard born in a place where the mother was not settled was to have its mother's place of settlement and the mother to be punished by a public whipping.

From 1844 a mother of an illegitimate child could apply to the justices for a maintenance order against the father.

It was only natural that many 'reputed' fathers would deny the accusation that they had sired an illegitimate child and an examination would then take place known as a 'bastardy examination'. These examinations are quite explicit in their content as the justices tried to determine exactly who was the father.

*Brampton Bastardy Examination for Elizabeth Crojer, singlewoman,
pregnant — 17 Nov 1820*

The justices' job was to find a father for a baseborn child and make him pay
a sum of money until the child was of an age to be apprenticed or put to
work and so relieve the parish of the responsibility of yet another poor child
in the parish. Over the years, some men would default in their payments and
these men will be shown on the calendars of prisoners in the local gaol on
bastardy charges. Some men would refuse to accept the justices' decision and
again, they will be found languishing in gaol. Of course, another solution to

Bastardy — A Bond of Indemnification, Purton, Wiltshire, dated 1713

the problem, sometimes by bribery, was to persuade the father of the child to marry the mother.

The papers to seek in bastardy cases are examinations and bastardy bonds.

The Poor Law
Until 1601 the relief of the poor was the responsibility of the church, but from this date it became the responsibility of the parish. The Poor Law Acts of 1601

and 1640 were the foundation of Poor Law administration for nearly 200 years, as described earlier in this chapter, but in the process of tracing a family history a resumé of events regarding the poor law is essential.

Many parishes had their own poor houses and from an act of 1722/3 parishes were encouraged to build or rent a workhouse which may have been only a poor hut on the common or waste land. If the parish did not provide the means for a poor house then paupers may have been billeted with other parishioners who had to take care of them. If a parish was too small or too poor to build its own poor house it was urged to unite with another parish to make it a viable proposition. Some parishes, it must be noted, were much more generous than others in dealing with their poor in that they would provide rent and food allowances and would even pay a doctor when necessary in addition to funeral expenses at the end of life; however, this only seemed to happen in the more affluent villages.

If a poor or workhouse was provided, not only adult paupers were sent to live there but young children and babies were also put into these places or sent out to nurse for a few pence a week. As a result of this cruel practice a Parliamentary Committee reported in 1715 that 'many poor infants are inhumanely suffered to die by the barbarity of the nurses who are a sort of people void of commiseration or religion hired by Churchwardens to take off a burden from the parish at the easiest rates they can and these know the manner of doing if efficiently'. Children who did survive this cruel practice would then be apprenticed at the early age of 7 years or so. If a vagrant couple with children should happen to trespass into a parish then their children could be apprenticed by the parish authorities against the will of the parents, once more relieving the parish of an intolerable burden.

By 1743/4 illegitimate children did not receive a settlement in the parish of their birth as formerly, but in their mother's parish of settlement and a person harbouring a vagrant could be heavily fined from ten shillings up to forty shillings.

Gilbert's Act of 1782 was an act which endeavoured to remedy the bad conditions existing in the workhouse, and to this end inspectors were appointed to conduct matters. Before Gilbert's Act, children could be separated from their parents but now children under 7 years of age were allowed to stay with their parents and paupers were not now to be sent to workhouses more than ten miles from their homes. Able-bodied poor were not allowed in the workhouse and at long last the humiliating practice of wearing paupers' badges were abolished, if they could prove they were of 'very decent and orderly behaviour'.

About 1795, the Speenhamland system of outdoor relief, which started in Speenhamland, Berkshire, was adopted and wages were made up to equal the cost of subsistence. This was based on a scale of relief for a family from the poor rate and the current price of bread. This system was adopted throughout the country but only had the effect that people now had enough to exist on and therefore did not want to work and maintain themselves. Gradually, through various unworkable and outmoded systems, we arrive at the year of 1834 and the Poor Law Amendment Act.

WARMINSTER UNION.
Common Charges.

LIST OF IRREMOVABLE POOR who have received OUT-DOOR RELIEF during the Half-Year ending March 26th, 1859.

DISTRICT No. 1.

Name of Pauper.	Age.	Where resident.	Belonging to	Cause of requiring Relief.	£.	s.	d.
Andrews, Sarah	51	Woodcock	Knooke	Her family	0	6	0
Biffin, William	26	King-street	Longbridge Deverill	Illness of himself	0	5	5
Bird, Sarah	63	West-street	Marston Bigot	Affliction	3	5	0
Bowns, Philip	61	Marsh-road	Norton Bavant	Cripple	3	18	0
Bowns, Edith	19	Ditto	Ditto	Afflicted	2	12	0
Bull, Henry	33	Bishopstrow	Westbury	Wife confined	0	8	0
Clarke, Jane	28	Furlong	Heytesbury	Illness of child	0	7	4
Carpenter, Jane	58	West-street	Horningsham	Affliction	3	0	11¼
Cockrell, Ann	50	Ash-walk	Chitterne All Saints	Ditto	4	19	1¼
Cornish, David	21	Cletherley	Warminster	Fits	2	7	11½
Cowdry, Jane	41	Bread-street	Heytesbury	Bedridden	4	4	0½
Cooper, John	22	Marsh	Longbridge Deverill	Illness of himself	0	14	9
Dicks, Jacob	74	Fore-street	Ditto	No work	3	7	1
Davis, Emmanuel	13	Workhouse	Heytesbury	For clothes	1	4	11
Davis, Maria	36	Bread-street	Imber	Husband in gaol	5	6	3
Davis, Ann	63	South-street	Ditto	Illness	2	18	11½
Bowns, Sarah	74	West-street	Corsley	Old age	2	18	8½
Dunford, William	77	Pound-street	Upton Scudamore	Ditto	3	13	11½
Exton, Richard	56	Warminster	Bishopstrow	Coffin for Mary	0	11	6
Exton, Robert	17	Ditto	Ditto	Illness	1	1	0
Exton, Matilda	23	South-street	Sutton Veny	Fits	0	9	2
Francis, Rebecca	49	West-street	Unknown	Her family	8	2	6
Franklyn, Jane	45	Pound-row	Westbury	Ditto	4	12	7½
Fry, Ann	28	Marsh-alley	Codford St. Peter	Illness	0	3	8
Garratt, George	22	West-street	Boyton	Ditto	5	4	9½
Garratt, Sarah	73	Imber-road	Horningsham	Old age	3	11	6
Grey, Jane	64	Smallbrook	Longbridge Deverill	No work	1	19	0
Hiskett, John	33	Pound-street	Ditto	Fits	3	18	7½
Hiskett, John, sen.	54	Bishopstrow	Sutton Veny	Illness of himself	6	1	10½
House, Sarah	50	Scotland	Heytesbury	Her family	2	3	10½
House, Elizabeth Jay.	19	Ditto	Ditto	Afflicted	2	7	6
Huld, Caroline	27	King-street	Frome	Husband a soldier	1	5	6½
Hurle, Edward	57	West-street	Ditto	Affliction	3	4	1½
King, Elizabeth	61	Borcham	Bishopstrow	No work	0	4	8
King, Eliza	37	Ditto	Ditto	Illness	2	16	4½
Laurence, Stephen	77	West-end	Longbridge Deverill	Old age	3	16	4½
Lloyd, Hester	75	Coldharbour	Westbury	Ditto	1	19	0
Marshall, Mary Ann	58	West-street	Unknown	No work	1	19	0
Miles, John	72	Chapel-street	Heytesbury	Blind	6	1	10½
Miles, Zilla	21	Ditto	Ditto	Confined	0	16	11½
Miller, Shadrach	44	Upton Scudamore	Westbury	Coffin for Timothy	0	7	7½
Nokes, Robert	73	Borcham-road	Heytesbury	Old age	0	10	0
Norris, John	35	Marsh-road	Bishopstrow	Boot & steel straps for child	1	10	0
Oram, Stephen	39	Hillwood	Sutton Veny	Wife confined	0	6	0

Poor Law — Warminster Union, Wiltshire — Outdoor Relief for Irremoveable Poor dated 1859

By 1834, the old poor law acts were amended and parishes were now encouraged to form into 'Unions'. Large workhouses were built to house paupers from a wider area and to contain those who were unable to support themselves. The responsibility of the parish for its poor was now transferred to the Union Workhouses under the Poor Law Unions, and Boards of Guardians were set up. Conditions were deliberately made as unpleasant as possible in an effort to encourage the poor to seek work and, to this end, employers were supposed to provide a living wage. More importance was placed on 'indoor' relief rather than 'outdoor' relief.

The work of the Guardians was closely and strictly supervised by the Poor Law Commission in London. Records had to be kept of all those in receipt of relief, outdoor or indoor, and often lists were printed and published. Records of admissions and other records are to be found in county record offices. Other minutes and reports made to the Commissioners in London are at the Public Record Office at Kew. Some 15,000 parishes were amalgamated into around 600 Unions. Similar systems were set up in Scotland in 1845 and in Ireland in 1833. The Guardians had to select a special and adequate diet from a list of supplied dietaries which contained specified amounts of solid food, enough to maintain the reasonable health of the inmates.

Conditions in the workhouse

Life was psychologically harsh for inmates of the workhouse as they were forced to wear standard pauper uniforms and the rules were that adults rose at 5 a.m. in summer and 7 a.m. in winter with work commencing at 7 a.m. or 8 a.m. to midday and from 1 p.m. to 6 p.m. with bedtime at 8 p.m. Women worked in the laundry or at other hard domestic tasks and men worked at whatever was available. The Workhouse Master enforced the rules of 'industry, order, punctuality and cleanliness' at all times. Husbands were separated from wives and children and they were not permitted to speak or communicate with one another, their meetings occurring at rare intervals and then only with the Guardians' permission. In turn, inmates were divided into various categories — 'aged or infirm' men and women; 'able-bodied' men and women over 16 years of age; boys or girls aged from 7 to 15 years; children under 7 years of age, all with their own living accommodation and exercise yards. Young children were usually allowed to stay with their mothers during any leisure time and to sleep with her at night. Children of pauper parents were to be apprenticed by the workhouse authorities although from 1844 education of workhouse children was provided.

All in all, the workhouse system was always open to abuse by the masters and mistresses in charge and residents had to abide by their rules and dictates. Although many poor were resident in the workhouse with its austere and forbidding conditions, many others were not resident but were 'relieved' by the poor rate and were known as the 'outdoor poor'.

The Poor Law Amendment Act of 1834 and other subsequent acts were eventually abolished under the Local Government Act of 1929 which transferred functions to Area Guardians Committees. The Poor Law finally came to an end with the National Assistance Act of 1948 and this act saw the closure of these miserable and unhappy places where many of our ancestors had existed.

Quarter session records and other records of the Clerk of the Peace

The Quarter Sessions were the courts of the Justices of the Peace for a county and were held from the fourteenth century until 1971 when they were abolished. Besides the Justices' jurisdiction over criminal matters they also had their administrative duties and were the governing bodies of counties

 *December 26th,* 1799

I N Order to prevent the false Reports maliciously circulated, setting forth that the Poor in the Work-House are STARVING, the following is a true Statement of the Provision allowed to *Ninety Four* Paupers, *Thirty-Five* and upwards of whom are Children under *Ten* years of age.

The Breakfasts are *Rice-Milk* and *Milk-Porridge*, alternately; the first is made with 32 pints of Milk, the same quantity of Water, 14 pounds of Rice, and one pound and half of Treacle, well seasoned. The *Milk-Porridge* consists of 32 pints of Milk, the same quantity of Water, seven pints of Oatmeal, and 20 pounds of Bread boiled together and seasoned with Salt, Pepper, &c.

The Dinners on *Sundays*, *Wednesdays*, and *Fridays*, are 40 pounds of Meat, and 84 pounds of Potatoes; the *Broth* of which is boiled on the same nights for Supper, with 36 pounds and a quarter of Bread, two pints of Oatmeal, with Onions, Salt, and Pepper.

On the other *Four* days, 24 pounds of Meat is cut in pieces and boiled with 30 pounds of Pease, made into Soup with Onions, &c. The Suppers on each of these nights are 36 pounds and a quarter of Bread, nine pounds and a quarter of Cheese, with good Table Beer.

Eight Paupers who do hard work, have an allowance of a quarter of a pound of Bread each, with Cheese and Beer, every working day at four o'clock; and Washer-Women have the same at eleven.

☞ *In order that the Poor may receive their due Portion of Diet, the Paupers choose from themselves weekly, an Inspector to see the Mistress weigh every Meal.*

T. SAUNDERS.

JOHN PAUL PAUL.

Circular issued from Tetbury, Gloucestershire, about the Workhouse Diet dated 1799

until reform in county administration by the Local Government Act of 1888 set up county councils to administer their affairs.

The records, therefore, deal not only with criminals but other persons in all walks of life and vary greatly in their content from county to county. The records will be found in the appropriate county record office.

Huntingdonshire Quarter Sessions — deposition of John Seaton dated 1839

Acts of Parliament throughout the centuries have given rise to innumerable documents relating to those in pursuance of their everyday lives and work. At all times, it must be realized that through the course of time certain records will have been thrown away by the clerk and his officers as being of no more use!

Justices of the Peace or magistrates were always of the gentry who dispensed summary justice where needed on wrong-doers, usually from their own homes, or sent them to prison to await trial at the Quarter Session courts held four times a year at designated places within a county at Hilary (Epiphany or Christmas); Easter; Trinity (Midsummer or St. Thomas); and Michaelmas. The magistrates received no remuneration for their duties.

It must be remembered in passing that magistrates with their comfortable way of life really had no conception of the lives led by their tenants and other poor and labouring families in their localities. As far as they were concerned God had decreed status on birth — the high and the low, and everyone knew their place in the scheme of things.

A well-known hymn by Mrs Alexander — *All Things Bright and Beautiful*, says it all:-

> The rich man in his castle
> The poor man at his gate
> God made them, high or lowly
> And order'd their estate.

Calendar of Prisoners in the county Bridewell, Huntingdon 1805

HUNTINGDON COUNTY GAOL.

11th Nov 1874

Particulars of a Person convicted of a Crime specified in the 20th Section of the Prevention of Crimes Act, 1871.

Name .... *Isaac Eddings*

and

Aliases ....

Age (on discharge) *13*

Height *4ft 9½*

Hair .... *Brown*

Eyes .... *Blue*

Complexion .... *Fresh*

Where born .... *Ramsey*

Married or single .... *Single*

Trade or occupation .... *Labourer*

Any other distinguishing mark ..... *Freckled about the face*

Description when liberated.

Photograph of Prisoner.

Address at time of apprehension .... *Kings Ripton Hunts*

Whether summarily disposed of or tried by a Jury. *Summarily*

Place and date of conviction .... *St Ives 26th Oct 1874*

Offence for which convicted .... *Stealing a Silver Watch*

Huntingdon County Gaol — Habitual Criminal Returns 1873-1878. For his crime Isaac received 21 day's hard labour, 8 strokes with a birch rod and 5 year's Reformatory

Judicial records are most comprehensive, and the main ones are:- The Great Rolls of Quarter Sessions, often existing from the sixteenth century or even before which included all the dealings of the court with returns of bailiffs, jury lists, indictments, depositions, presentments, calendars of prisoners, removal orders which were the subject of appeal, recognizances, etc. At times, some papers will be found in separate bundles or lists such as the calendars of prisoners, removal orders, insolvent debtors, and process and order books.

In the records of the Clerk of the Peace will be found a wealth of documentation which will add to the knowledge of your ancestors' backgrounds and their way of life.

From a seemingly endless list here follows a typical selection of sources:-

- Oaths of allegiance, declarations and scarament certificates. A series of acts commencing with the Test Act of 1672 necessitated the taking of various oaths. This act required all persons taking public office, with the exception of minor civil offices, to take oaths of allegiance and supremacy and to provide evidence that they had received the Sacrament according to the custom of the Church of England. This was mainly directed against protestant dissenters; however Roman Catholics or papists were further excluded as they had to make a declaration denying transubstantiation, an essential part of Roman Catholic doctrine. This type of record appears up to around the middle of the nineteenth century.

- Numerous societies were obliged to register with the Clerk, these were mainly friendly societies, freemasons, and printing presses as well as saving banks. Certificates and lists of freemsons had to be submitted under the Unlawful Societies Act of 1799 and there are certificates and registers with members', names, addresses, occupations, under the name of their lodges. Likewise, all those who operated printing presses had to register under the same act.

- Summary convictions and depositions include a number of registers which, at times, were kept separately from the Quarter Session Great Rolls such as registers of convictions for poaching; convictions and returns of juvenile offenders under fourteen years of age; the swearing of profane oaths; selling beer without a licence; assault; offences against the game laws.

- Bonds and contracts for transportation of felons to the American colonies and elsewhere.

- Registers and deputations of gamekeepers and certificates under various acts commencing with the Game Laws from 1710.

- Copies of vagrants' passes and examinations sent to the Clerk of the Peace; bastardy returns and removals.

- Hair Powder Duty certificates for persons using hair powder. Under an Act of 1794/5, all those using hair powder had to obtain an annual certificate by paying a duty of one guinea — these certificates and registers include names of servants who were also obliged to use hair powder by their employers.

- Licensed victuallers with enrolled recognizances for good order and government of alehouses.

- Badgers, so called because they wore a badge to show they had been licensed by the justices to sell corn and other victuals, also known as laders, kidders, and carriers. Cattle drovers had to apply for a licence to trade as well as badgers. The licences and registers show names, occupations, abode, sureties, and the date of the Quarter sessions in which they applied and were granted their licences dating from 1551/2 until 1772.

- Provisions were made for the killing, dressing and selling of meat in Lent and on fast days and licences were needed for this by butchers.

- Returns of parish constables under the Parish Constables Act of 1842 until around 1862, despite the fact that county police forces were to be set up under the County Police Act of 1839.
- County Police forces sent in monthly returns of disposition and numbers and admission registers with names of constables, their description, where born, and, if married, the wife's birth place, may be found in this collection.
- Militia accounts of payments to the overseers for relief of militia men and their families, lists of militia men and rolls of militia substitutes.
- Lists of persons qualified to serve on juries.
- Turnpike Trusts: Repair of Highways: Bridges: Inspection of Woollen mills and other factories: Recruitment of Army and Navy under the Navy Acts of 1794/5 with names of men enrolled; Maimed soldiers' petitions: Hearth Tax papers from 1662: Registers of barges under the Defence Acts of 1798 and 1803: Licensing of private asylums with certificates of admissions, removals, discharges, deaths and abscondences: Returns of pauper and criminal lunatics: Poll books: Registers of Electors from 1832: Coroners' inquisitions and bills which were submitted for fees and travelling expenses with brief details of the inquisitions with names, dates, places and cause of death — these are closed to the public for seventy-five years, as are, usually, asylum records. (see also Chapter 11 — Newspapers for Coroners' inquests).
- In 1971, the office of Clerk of the Peace and Assize Courts were abolished as well as Courts of Quarter Sessions.

One often neglected source is the Enrolled Deeds under a statute of 1535/6 which stated that no transfer of land by bargain or sale was to take place unless the indenture was enrolled with the Clerk of the Peace. These deeds can give an indication of an ancestor's place of residence together with family names and can give leads back in time, in some cases, before the commencement of parish registers, or may confirm ancestry in a certain place.

Other series of documents include Enclosure awards, conveyances by turn-pike trustees of toll houses, land and other properties, including turnpike road maps, parish agreements for the erection of workhouses, etc.

Another source are the Land Tax Assessments from the late eighteenth century (see Chapter 3). These extensive records of the Clerk of the Peace and Quarter Sessions lead to a different but fascinating area of research for the genealogist. Many county record offices publish guides to these particular records and it is wise to enquire about them before contemplating any work in this area of family history.

It must be stressed that although Assizes were held within each county to hear and judge any major crimes sent on from the justices in sessions, the assize records will *not* be found in county records at all but are termed national records and, as such, are held in the Public Record Office, Chancery Lane, London, with all their appropriate documentation (see Chapter 13).

The Assizes for London and Middlesex were termed 'special jurisdictions' and before 1834 sessions were held before the Lord Mayor. The surviving records for the City of London are in the Corporation of London Record Office,

Guildhall, London, EC2P 2EJ, and those for Middlesex are in the Greater London Record Office, 40 Northampton Road, London, EC1R 0HB. From 1834 until the abolition of assizes, the Central Criminal Court at the Old Bailey served as the assize court for London, Middlesex, and parts of Essex, Kent, and Surrey. From 1834 these records are held in the Public Record Office, Chancery Lane, London.

Courts of Great Sessions for Wales from the sixteenth century to 1830 are held in the National Library of Wales, Aberystwyth. Other records may be found in the appropriate Welsh record offices.

Some interesting extracts from Wiltshire Quarter Sessions records of the 17th century

1610 The Constables of the Borough of Wilton present Benjamin Salisbury who was indicted and convicted for 'an incorrigible rogue' and by the judgement of the court was ordered to be burned on the left shoulder with a letter 'R' and to remain in gaol till he find good sureties for his good behaviour.

1632 Andrew Washbeard of Porton presented 'for keeping and maintaining of an unruly mastif dog to the great terror and prejudice of all the neighbours and to all passengers who have occasion to travel that way'.

1639 The Jury for the hundred of Whorlesdown present that Samuel Brown is a drunkard and that John Newman of Tinhead sold beer without a licence under the pretence of a wine licence.

1646 Robert Poope by the consent of the constables and overseers and the rest of the inhabitants of Potterne for beere and tobacco for the use of sicke people in the time of sickness £7. 9s. 0d.

1647 Edward Farley was presented (of Heytesbury) for disturbing of the Minister during the time of divine service.

1677 Richard Cousins kept an unlawful game of skittles and William Wansborough kept an unlawful game by playing skittles.

Coroners' Bills for the 18th century

1774 Ann Swain, starved and murdered by Stephen Swain her father and Tamar his wife. (The case went to the Assizes and the couple were hanged).

1775 Robert Allen otherwise Chap, a vagrant rambling from place to place, infested with vermin, died in an outhouse.

1775 Alexander Applegarth, swallowed over three pints of distilled spirits called brandy and rum, instantly killed himself.

1780 Elizabeth Jones being conveyed by a pass from Basingstoke, Hants to Corsham, died on the road.

1783 The Roebuck Inn in Preshute beyond Marlborough, Thomas Griffiths killed by the overturning of the coach he was

driving from the snow and badness of the weather in Marlborough Forest.

Comments

- The Overseers of the Poor accounts often show items such as 'badges' at
one penny or halfpenny each. These are the badges which paupers were
forced to wear on their clothing — a large 'P' followed by the initial letter
of the name of the parish, for example, a pauper from Faringdon in Berkshire would have a badge 'PF'. Penalties for disobeying this could result
in loss of relief and even imprisonment in the local bridewell.
- Tradesmen would be employed to work on the parish roads by the Sur-
veyor of the Highways, and accounts will often show what trade an ancestor followed.
- Other documentation concerning the incumbent of a parish will be found
in diocesan papers.
- If an apprentice was ill-treated by a master or mistress, that employer could
be taken in front of the magistrates and the apprentice discharged and re-
apprenticed elsewhere and the master punished. Certificates of discharge
may be found in Quarter Session records, parish or civil records. If an apprentice ran away from his master, warrants would be issued for his or her
arrest — these may be found in the records of the Clerk of the Peace.
- Settlements, examinations and removals may be found in some cases as
late as the second half of the nineteenth century.
- If a husband deserted his wife and family, a warrant could be issued for
his apprehension. These warrants may be found in parish, civil or quarter
session records.
- Some workhouse papers contain lists of births and baptisms in the workhouse. Many of these births were of illegitimate children and a private baptism could well have been the only baptism which may, or may not have
been recorded in the parish register by the incumbent who was responsible
for the workhouse and its inmates.
- Burial lists of workhouse inmates may be in workhouse papers.
- Some Boards of Guardians had a system of inoculation for smallpox, and
records were kept of these with names and ages.
- If a workhouse inmate absconded in the workhouse uniform a warrant would
be issued by the magistrates for his apprehension.

Further reading

County Records by F.G. Emmison and Irvine Gray (Historical Association 1973).
Archives and Local History by F.G. Emmison (Phillimore 1978).
Enjoying Archives by David Iredale (Phillimore 1985).
Local Historians' Encyclopedia by John Richardson (Historical Publications
1986).
A History of English Assizes 1558-1714 by J.S. Cockburn (Cambridge 1972).
Quarter Session Records for Family Historians — a select list compiled by J.S.W.
Gibson (Second Ed. FFHS 1986).

The Poor Law in Nineteenth-century England and Wales by Anne Digby (Historical Association).

The Old Poor Law 1795-1834 by J.D. Marshall (1985).

The Village Labourer by J.L. and Barbara Hammond (Longman P/B 1978).

Illegitimacy by Eve McLaughlin (FFHS 1985).

Annals of the Poor by Eve McLaughlin (FFHS 1986).

The Parish Chest by W.E. Tate (Phillimore).

Churchwardens Accounts by J.C. Cox (1913).

Coroners Records in England and Wales by J. Gibson and C. Rogers (FFHS 1988).

My Ancestor was a Migrant by A.J. Camp (Society of Genealogists).

CHAPTER 8

County Record Offices (CRO)

The majority of County Record Offices were not established until after the Second World War. Their function is to preserve, restore, and make available for public viewing, the archives, not only of their own particular district, but in some cases, of a wider area as well. A good example of this is that a CRO will often hold such records as Manorial documents, wills, and copies of the IGI for areas other than their own.

Mainly, the first deposits in record offices were those of the Clerk of the Peace, Quarter Session rolls, and manorial rolls. Gradually, throughout the years, county record offices have acquired more and more archives. Many Diocesan Record Offices have now closed and the ecclesiastical documents peculiar to these types of offices have now found their way into the appropriate county record office. For the genealogist, the county record office is a positive 'treasure trove' for here will be found, not only parish registers and parish records, but a vast amount of other archival material which enables the researcher to explore practically every aspect of family history.

All offices have rules and regulations concerning their material and it is wise to enquire about facilities and opening hours of search rooms before contemplating a visit. Most county record offices publish leaflets and guides to their holdings and these are always worth reading. The following list is a fairly typical one for any county, but of course collections vary from area to area.

- Records of the Clerk of the Peace: Quarter; Petty, Special and Brewster Sessions.
- County Councils: Local Authorities: Urban and Rural District Councils.
- Union Workhouses and Board of Guardians (Admissions; minutes; birth and death registers, payments to outside poor, etc.).
- Solicitors' records.
- Family and Estate archives.
- Manorial records.
- Business; Factory and Industrial archives.

- Schools:- Charity, Board, Church of England, Sunday School, and Local Education Authority (LEA).
- County Police Force.
- Militia.
- Barges and Canals.
- Land and other taxes.
- Poll books and Electoral registers.
- Tithe maps and Awards.
- Enclosure maps and Awards.
- Wills and administrations.
- Banns books, marriage licences, bonds and allegations.
- National Trust.
- Charities.
- Leases and Deeds.
- Hospitals and Asylums.
- Prisons.
- Ancient town, city, and borough records.
- Newspapers.
- Maps.
- Diocesan records.
- Parish Registers; Parish Records; Bishops' Transcripts.

Diocesan records

These are the documents and records which need to be undertaken in the light of more advanced research when most other sources have been looked at and exhausted. Generally, most Diocesan Record Offices have now been absorbed into County Record Offices but a few still operate as separate establishments.

The records contained in the collection of this office are those connected with the ecclesiastical authorities such as Archdeacons, Bishops, Deans, and other officials of the church courts and authorities. We have already dealt with Bishops' Transcripts, marriage licence bonds and allegations, wills before 1858 and glebe terriers in other chapters, and these are part of the diocesan archives.

It must be pointed out that many of these documents may not have yet been indexed and catalogued or are only in the process of being dealt with by archivists, and it is wise to make enquiries from your record office to find out if they have any guides to these particular records. Diocesan records, therefore, are those of a diocesan registry and are concerned with the everyday workings of the ecclesiastical courts such as those already mentioned. Documentation dates from around the fifteenth century, with some from before then, and deals with all matters appertaining to church business and offences against the church or canon law.

In these archives will be found:
- Will disputes known as 'Testamentary causes'.

- Non-observance of the Lord's Day or Holy days and non-attendance at church.
- Non-payments of Easter tithes or Easter offerings.
- Parish dues.
- Returns of papists with names and abodes.
- Glebe Terriers.
- Confirmation lists.
- State of church fabric and buildings.
- Churchwardens and Clergy presentments.
- Bishops Act books.
- Behaviour of minister and parish officials.
- Licencing of clergy, schoolmasters, midwives and surgeons.
- Conduct of parishioners in and around the church.
- Betrothal and marriage; separations.
- Slander, defamation of character, fornication, adultery, blasphemy, breach of promise — many of these last named stem from the churchwardens' 'presentments' when they presented to the Archdeacon or Bishop as to whether all was well with the church, parish, and parishioners or to report if anything had been amiss since the last presentation. Woe betide anyone who had offended, such as a girl or even a widow having an illegitimate child; a couple who had committed fornication before marriage or adultery, or anyone who had gossiped maliciously about their neighbour, for they all would appear on the presentment. The church correctional courts would then set to work on these offences, imposing punishments, penances, and excommunications on the offending parties.

Penances generally would be carried out in the local parish church in the presence of the congregation during divine service, occasionally some were allowed, for some reason or another, to perform their penance privately. Excommunications could exact a penance in some extreme cases by six months in gaol, and excommunications could be lifted after a period of time by confession, prayer and the payment of a fee.

Certificates may be found in these records stating what kind of penance had to be performed and are found in what are known as 'Correction' books or 'Comperta and Detecta' books. Summons were drawn up in 'Citation' books in which will be found cases of immorality, marriage, probate, church finance, unlicensed teachers, midwives, and the like.

- There may have been a dispute amongst a family about a will or administration and these 'testamentary causes' will be found in diocesan archives.
- If a couple wanted to separate, the church courts would sit in judgement and decide whether it was possible, and documents will be found with depositions, statements from both parties and innumerable witnesses giving testimonies. In fact, these marital separation procedures usually dragged on for a number of years. (see Chapter 12, Divorce).

It must be admitted that these archives are often overlooked even by the more experienced family historian but it is advisable to bear this type of record in mind and explore an avenue of genealogy where there is a fascinating diversity of material awaiting.

One of the many examples I have found for my own family was the instance when my ancestor, Barbara Tanner married a George Gosse, and on trying to find her baptism I came across two Barbara Tanners being baptised in two parishes some miles apart, one in 1604 and one in 1608 — so, which Barbara was mine? They languished in my files for some years until one day, searching through 'testamentary causes' I came across a law suit regarding a will dated 1639 where a Barbara Gosse, wife of George Gosse was giving a statement. Her testimony stated she had lived in the parish of Sandford for fifteen years from the date of her marriage and that she was 35 years of age, thus proving to me that the Barbara Tanner baptised in the neighbouring parish of Witheridge in 1604 was, indeed, my Barbara Tanner. As almost all wills for Devon were destroyed by bombing during the Second World War, this was my only means of proving which Barbara was my ancestor.

Here are some other typical entries from the records:-

A William Betteridge was summoned to the vestry room of his parish church and in front of Ann Edlen whose character he had defamed, together with her friends and witnesses, made a recantation, afterwards certifying in the Cathedral church on the 26 July 1792 between the hours of 9 a.m. and 12 noon, that he had carried out this penance.

Another interesting document found was a pew dispute in 1792 between two men with one saying the pew belonged to him as he occupied the estate to whom the pew belonged for seven years. The other man's wife stated that she had sat in that pew when she was an apprentice girl for 41 years previously. Unfortunately, for her, the person who had occupied the estate was entitled to sit in the pew.

A poor girl, in a seventeenth century document, was 'presented' by the churchwardens of her parish to the Archdeacon, for having an illegitimate child. To absolve herself of this crime she was to stand in front of the congregation all through divine service attired in a white sheet, bare headed, bare-legged and with bare feet holding a white rod an ell long. When the Vicar summoned her she had to beg for forgiveness of her neighbours and promise she would not commit the like offence again, begging the congregation to join her in the Lord's prayer

One October day in 1757, one Mary New defamed the character of Elizabeth Elkins, a spinster, and Mary was summoned to appear before the court to be judged for her actions and apologize to Elizabeth. This, Mary refused to do and was excommunicated. Obviously, a woman who knew her own mind! These types of documents appear mainly up to the seventeenth century and in some cases to the eighteenth century, and early nineteenth century.

Not many books have been written on this aspect of history but *The Parish Chest* by W.E. Tate, devotes a chapter to this kind of record. Some Bishops' registers and books have been printed for some dioceses giving an interesting insight into Diocesan archives.

Further reading

The Parish Chest by W.E. Tate (Phillimore).

Church Treasury of History, Custom and Folklore by W. Andrews (1898).

Curious Church Customs by W. Andrews (1895).

In and Around Record Offices in Great Britain and Ireland by Rosemary Church and Jean Cole (Wiltshire FHS 1987).

Record Offices and how to find them by J.S.W. Gibson and Pamela Peskett (FFHS 1987).

Phillimore's Atlas & Index (Phillimore).

County Records by F.G. Emmison & Irvine Gray (Historical Association 1983).

Tracing your Family History by Jean Cole (Family Tree Publications 1988).

Enjoying Archives by David Iredale (Phillimore 1985).

Local London Archives (Greater London Archives Network 1985).

How to Locate and Use Manorial Records by Patrick Palgrave-Moore (Elvery Dowers 1985).

Wills before 1858 by Eve McLaughlin (FFHS 1986).

Probate Jurisdiction by J.S.W. Gibson (FFHS 1986).

Bishops Transcripts and Marriage Licences by J.S.W. Gibson (FFHS 1986).

Quarter Sessions Records by J.S.W. Gibson (FFHS 1986).

Census Returns on Microfilm by J.S.W. Gibson (FFHS 1986).

Hearth Tax, other Later Stuart Tax Lists and the Association Oath Rolls by J.S.W. Gibson (FFHS 1986).

Annals of the Poor by Eve McLaughlin (FFHS 1987).

Illegitimacy by Eve McLaughlin (FFHS 1986).

Parish Registers by Eve McLaughlin (FFHS 1986).

CHAPTER 9

The Church of Jesus Christ of Latter Day Saints (Mormons) and the International Genealogical Index, or the IGI

The Church of Jesus Christ of Latter Day Saints was founded in 1830 by Joseph Smith, who claimed in 1827, after seeing a series of visions, he had discovered a set of gold plates engraved with a revelation which, with the help of two heavenly messengers, was translated from 'reformed Egyptian' into English. This is the book described as the *Book of Mormon,* published in 1830, and from this the members of the church also became known as Mormons.

At this time, a small group of followers who accepted his testimony was formed in New York at Fayette. Smith was an eloquent preacher who influenced many people but he was often in trouble with the authorities, constantly being turned out from one place after another, until he ended up in Illinois. Smith's murder in 1844 made him a martyr in the eyes of the Mormon church, and his place was taken by Brigham Young, an exceptional leader, who stamped out warring factions and helped to enlarge and popularize the Church. Young announced to the faithful that he had a revelation to lead them to the Great Salt Lakes — a trek of over 1,000 miles over rough and desert country. Many of the faithful made this terrible journey only with handcarts. After many vicissitudes they finally arrived in the valley of the Great Salt Lake in 1847 and here they built their church and communities. By 1850, 30,000 Mormons reached their Promised Land and Brigham Young ruled and directed the affairs of the Church until his death thirty years later in 1877. Polygamy was one of the Mormon doctrines, and this brought the sect into disrepute until the practice was finally renounced in 1890. Mormons believe that some time Jesus Christ will appear and rule for 1,000 years.

Although the Church of Jesus Christ of Latter Day Saints was founded in America, there were many converts from all over the world, some making the journey to Utah during the early days of the Church, whilst others remained in their own countries founding churches to extend the religion.

The IGI - What is it?
The International Genealogical Index, formerly called the Computer File Index, is one of the most useful tools available for the genealogical researcher. It

makes copies of parish register entries available practically anywhere in the world. For this, family historians are indebted to the Church of Jesus Christ of Latter Day Saints.

It is part of the Mormon doctrine that families should be joined together in one unit, and church members trace their long dead ancestors, who are then ceremoniously baptized into the faith. Mormon missionaries are despatched to record repositories to copy register entries, usually for baptisms and marriages. In the early days much opposition was encountered from churches and chapels, and in many cases Mormons were not even allowed on the premises. Generally, now, these barriers are being broken down and more and more registers are copied each year. Not all the entries on the files are taken from parish records, some are notes and entries of items such as wills sent into the church, not only by its own members, but by the general public.

The IGI covers not just British records, but it is almost world-wide. One has to remember that America is known as the 'melting pot' of the world, and US citizens have ancestry from many non-English speaking countries. The Index is subdivided into counties and states as far as Britain and the US is concerned. Other separate areas include Scotland, Wales, Ireland, the Channel Islands and the Isle of Man. Besides the European area, over 70 other countries are covered.

The Index is updated every few years and is on microfiche. The films are sold by the church and as a consequence they are available for viewing in places such as Public Record Offices, libraries and other repositories. The Mormon church has a number of genealogical libraries in Britain, and a full list of addresses may be obtained by sending an S.A.E. to The Genealogical Library, The Church of Jesus Christ of Latter Day Saints, 64-68 Exhibition Road, London, SW7 2PA. Any films not in stock at a branch may be ordered and are quickly despatched from the largest genealogical library in the world at Salt Lake City. Besides the IGI they hold a vast collection of wills, census returns and other genealogical material on microfilm and fiche.

There is no fee for using the libraries, but a small charge is made for photo-copies of the frames, and a donation towards their running costs is always appreciated. The records at Salt Lake City are stored in huge man-made vaults, excavated 700ft deep into the granite mountains. They are kept at a constant 57-60° F, and humidity is controlled to 40-50 per cent. It is said the capacity is equal to 26 million, 300 page volumes.

How to read it

At the top of each frame there is the name of the country and county, the date of the release, e.g. as of July 1984, and the page number. Next we see the surname and christian name of the recorded person. By the side of this is the name of the father, mother, and spouse. After this we see two narrow columns, the first having letters that represent M = male; F = female; H = husband; W = wife. In the second of the two narrow columns you will see

COUNTRY: ENGLAND	COUNTY: DERBY				AS OF JUL 1984			PAGE 392	
NAME	(SEX M MALE F FEMALE-H HUSBAND W WIFE)		EVENT	TOWN, PARISH	B	E	S	SOURCE BATCH	SERIAL SHEET
	FATHER-MOTHER OR SPOUSE		DATE						
ARMSTRONG, THOMAS									
ARMSTRONG, THOMAS	THOMAS ARMSTRONG/HANNAH	M C	24AUG1823	ALFRETON	06MAR1976MZ	13MAR1976MZ	14APR1976MZ	C046271	1291
ARMSTRONG, THOMAS	RICHARD ARMSTRONG/HANNAH	M C	31OCT1824	DERBY,SAINT ALKMUND KING STREET-W SLETAN METHODIST	14JAN1978AL	09MAR1976AL	29MAR1978AL	C066661	0489
ARMSTRONG, THOMAS	THOMAS ARMSTRONG/HANNAH	M C	26FEB1832	ALFRETON	06MAR1976MZ	18MAR1976MZ	16APR1976MZ	C046271	2574
ARMSTRONG, THOMAS	GEORGE ARMSTRONG/JANE	M C	12FEB1833	DERBY,SAINT WERBURGH	04JUN1976OG	07SEP1976OG	21OCT1976OG	C049861	7538
ARMSTRONG, THOMAS		M C	04MAR1836	GLOSSOP,NEW MILLS-WESLEYAN	02NOV1977SL	26NOV1977SL	17FEB1978SL	C066751	0090
ARMSTRONG, THOMAS	SAMUEL ARMSTRONG/MARIA WOOLLEY CHARLOTTE RAINS	H M	11OCT1841	NORTH WINGFIELD		22AUG1978SL	N058751	0554
ARMSTRONG, THOMS	MARTHA LOW	H M	10JAN1771	NORTH WINGFIELD		02NOV1978OG	N058752	0681
ARMSTRONG, THOS.	RUTH CUIT	H M	19OCT1704	BLACKWELL BY ALFRETON		04JAN1972SG	7106033	76
ARMSTRONG, WALTER		H C	28NOV1869	HEATH	20MAY1981SE	30JUL1981SE	15SEP1981SE	C055093	0665
	GEORGE ARMSTRONG/ELIZABETH				02NOV1977SL				
ARMSTRONG, WALTON	JANE ARMSTRONG	H C	27MAR1844	CHESTERFIELD	29APR1977PV	13JUN1977PV	UNCLEARED	C035862	9869
ARMSTRONG, WILLIAM		H C	11FEB1731	BOLSOVER	15MAR1979OG	18MAY1979OG	01JUN1979OG	C060972	0992
	WILLIAM ARMSTRONG/BRIDGET								
ARMSTRONG, WILLIAM	MARY LOWE	H M	01JUN1734	CHAPEL EN LE FRITH		09APR1984SL	A184796	4780
ARMSTRONG, WILLIAM	MARY LOWE	H M	01JUN1734	CHAPEL EN LE FRITH		18JUN1973LG	7230730	32
ARMSTRONG, WILLIAM	ELIZABETH BEANE	H M	29NOV1748	SUTTON CUM DUCKMANTON		05JAN1982LG	N059402	0147
ARMSTRONG, WILLIAM	MARTHA BOULSOVER	H C	09AUG1756	BOLSOVER		22JAN1981OK	C060972	0174
ARMSTRONG, WILLIAM	SARAH YEOMANS	H M	12AUG1762	CHESTERFIELD		10NOV1978LA	M035863	3040
ARMSTRONG, WILLIAM	WM ARMSTRONG/MARTHA	H C	06FEB1768	BOLSOVER	15MAR1979OG	18MAY1979OG	05JUN1979OG	C060972	1709
ARMSTRONG, WILLIAM	BENJN ARMSTRONG/MARY	H C	07MAR1768	BOLSOVER	15MAR1979OG	18MAY1979OG	05JUN1979OG	C060972	1710
ARMSTRONG, WILLIAM	CATHERINE JACKSON	H M	14APR1789	BOLSOVER		22JAN1981OK	C060972	0447
ARMSTRONG, WILLIAM	BENJN ARMSTRONG/MARY	H C	21OCT1795	BOLSOVER	15MAR1979OG	19MAY1979OG	01JUN1979OG	C060972	2812
ARMSTRONG, WILLIAM	RUTH MITCHEL	H M	18APR1814	BOLSOVER		19OCT1977PV	N060971	0017
ARMSTRONG, WILLIAM	MARGARET CHAPMAN	H C	07OCT1823	CHESTERFIELD		23AUG1977WA	M035862	0923
ARMSTRONG, WILLIAM		H C	19OCT1824	BOLSOVER	24AUG1977WA	26OCT1977WA	12NOV1977WA	C060971	0490
	WILLIAM ARMSTRONG/MARGARET								
ARMSTRONG, WILLIAM	WILLIAM ARMSTRONG/MARY	H M	09APR1827	CRICH	22MAY1976MT	14AUG1976MT	31AUG1976MT	C049781	1456
ARMSTRONG, WILLIAM	THOMAS ARMSTRONG/HANNAH	H C	03JAN1830	ALFRETON	06MAR1976MZ	17MAR1976MZ	16APR1976MZ	C046271	2269
ARMSTRONG, WILLIAM	WILLIAM ARMSTRONG/RUTH	H C	16MAY1831	HEATH	17JUL1976LA	07OCT1976LA	13OCT1976LA	C055091	0245
ARMSTRONG, WILLIAM	SARAH ADAMS	H M	12AUG1833	MELBOURNE		13OCT1977SL	M055591	0863
ARMSTRONG, WILLIAM		H C	29JUN1850	BOLSOVER	24AUG1977WA	27OCT1977WA	15NOV1977WA	C060971	1569
	BENJAMIN ARMSTRONG/ELIZA								
ARMSTRONG, WILLIAM #	ELIZABETH RATCLIFFE	H M	09JUN1851	ALFRETON		CLEARED		N046273	0858
ARMSTRONG, WILLIAM HENRY		H C	16NOV1862	STAVELEY	15SEP1976AZ	18DEC1976AZ	03FEB1977AZ	C055751	5654
	MATTHEW ARMSTRONG/JANE								
ARMSTRONG, WILLIAM JOHN		H C	20JUL1862	BOLSOVER	24AUG1977WA	27OCT1977WA	17NOV1977WA	C060971	2004
	JAMES ARMSTRONG/MARY								
ARMSTRONG, WM	BENJ ARMSTRONG/ANN	H M	18MAR1748	BOLSOVER	15MAR1979OG	18MAY1979OG	01JUN1979OG	C060972	1206
ARMSTRONG, WM	JOHN ARMSTRONG/ANN	H M	18MAY1789	AULT HUCKNALL	20JUN1974SL	17SEP1974SL	22NOV1974SL	7405302	47
ARMSTRONG, WM	WM ARMSTRONG/CATHARINE	H C	13JUN1800	BOLSOVER	15MAR1979OG	19MAY1979OG	01JUN1979OG	C060972	3032
	JOHN ARMSTRONG/MARY								
ARMSTRONG, WM.		H M	18MAY1789	AULT HUCKNALL	26FEB1976PV	08APR1976PV	20MAY1976PV	C048271	0714
=ARMSTRONGE , ** SEE ARMSTRONG									
*ARMSWORTH									
ARMSWORTH, WM.	HANNAH WILSON	H M	08FEB1751	EYAM		03MAR1976LG	7518115	22
=ARNALL , ** SEE ARNOLD									
=ARNAT , ** SEE ARNOT									
=ARNATI , ** SEE ARNOT									
*ARNAUD									
ARNAUD, BENJAMIN	BENJAMIN ARNAUD/ELIZA	H C	10OCT1824	THORPE BY ASHBOURNE	04FEB1977MT	06APR1977MT	10MAY1977MT	C058991	0082
=ARNAULD , ** SEE ARNOLD									
=ARNE , ** SEE ARNET									
=ARNEFIELD , ** SEE ARNFIELD									
=ARNEL , ** SEE ARNOLD									

Printout from the Mormon International Genealogical Index (IGI)

another letter, A = adult christening; B = birth; C = christening; D = death or burial; F = birth or christening of first known child; M = marriage; N = census; W = will, and all others are miscellaneous entries. These columns are followed by the date of the event, and next comes the town or parish. The contents of the final five columns look, and are, rather complicated. They are not generally of interest to most researchers, being more helpful to members of the LDS Church. Here is an example of one line taken from the IGI for Derbyshire as of July 1984:-

ARMSTRONG, THOMAS	THOMAS ARMSTRONG/HANNAH	M	C	24 AUG 1823	ALFRETON

This tells us that a male child was christened on 24 August 1823 at Alfreton, Derbyshire and was the son of Thomas and Hannah Armstrong. All very simple, straightforward and easy to understand. As mentioned earlier the IGI is far from a complete list of parish records, but it is an extremely helpful research tool. Another point worth remembering is that like all other human transcriptions, inaccuracies can arise, so check all your entries with the originals when you get the chance.

Further reading
General Register Office and International Genealogical Indexes. Where to find them by J.S.W. Gibson (FFHS).

CHAPTER 10

Manorial Records

We have to rely largely upon the records of the Manorial system if we are to find our way before the beginning of Parish records. The chances of tracing your family in an unbroken line from the time of the Domesday period of 1086, let alone that of the actual invasion of England by William, of Normandy, is very remote, but not altogether impossible. You stand more chance of achieving such a target if you are lucky enough to have connected yourself to one of the landowning gentry lines of that period.

Soon after the annex of the natives of these shores by William and his fellow invaders, very few of the ruling classes in Britain were other than Norman sympathisers. The Manorial system became the equivalent of a local government, but instead of elected representatives of the people as we have now, the Lord of the Manor was the head of the court, answerable to the King, but wielding great power over the lives of residents of the unit. It was not altogether a local dictatorship, for there was a rough and ready, but relatively effective system of law and order, which even the Lord of the Manor was expected to observe. The residents were divided into various social classes, each person knowing his own place.

The villein, an unfree tenant, was very much under the will of the Lord. He held land, but was given very few privileges. He was allowed to graze his cattle on the common, and also collect hay and firewood. He was not, however, able to acquire land without it being taxed, nor even let his daughter marry without the Lord's permission. When a villein died, a fine (heriot) was levied. He paid the Lord a rent for his land, usually in kind or by working part of the time for him. Gradually, especially after the Black Death, largely due to the decrease in population, the villein was able to improve his position on the social scale.

A status even lower than the villein existed in the early days — that of the serf. He was just a servant to the Lord and could be bought and sold like a slave. It was possible for the Lord to give freedom to a serf and grant him a small area of land, but nothing like the size of the villein's holding. A cottar was another name for this class of person.

A Freeholder was a landowner, who, although paying rent to the Lord, was not obliged to carry out any of the feudal tasks.

There were various other names and classes, but here we are just trying to make the explanations as simple as possible. The administration of law and order as we know it today, has largely evolved from the Manorial system, and it is mostly from these records that we may be lucky enough to obtain details of our ancestors.

The communal judicial system is best simply described as two separate systems, the court leet and the court baron, which, at times, functioned as one. Every manor had to hold a court baron, to ensure the manor operated in the manner prescribed by the Crown. This was a court at which the tenants were obliged to attend. It presided over such things as transfers and surrenders of land, the management of common land and the rights of the Lord of the Manor and his tenants. It was not necessary to hold a court leet. Although many manors did hold these separately, others held them at the same time as the Court Baron. The court leet dealt with the many minor offences.

There was a delegation of responsibilities by the Lord of the Manor to various people to enable the system to run as smoothly as possible. A Steward was appointed. His responsibility lay in the keeping of the records of events taking place in the manor. He held the court and assured that the conveyancing of land was carried out correctly.

A Bailiff was an overseer to the estate who was appointed by the Steward; he was often referred to as the Steward's Manager. He was usually responsible for the announcement of the court meetings, and at times, even recorded the events for the Steward. The Reeve was responsible for arranging the duties the tenants were obliged to do for the Lord; he was elected by the villeins and was usually a member of that class. He was paid for his duties by the copy-holders themselves. A Hayward was responsible for the general repair of such things as hedges and fences around the manor. It was he who rounded up stray cattle and impounded them in the pinfold, and he also acted as agent for the Lord concerning the sale of corn and other similar commodities. The Constable's duty, then as now, was to keep the peace. It was an annual appointment, which also required the holder to summon the jurors to serve in the courts.

All this is a rather simplified account of the system. The condition of the records varies from area to area. As with all other records, some were better kept than others and many are missing altogether.

The information to be gleaned from manor rolls depends much on the general activities of its residents. You should be able to learn the names of the jurors called to serve in the courts, and also the officials. If your ancestor died, a record would perhaps have been made of a fine imposed if his land was transferred.

Perhaps your ancestor committed one of the many crimes that warranted his appearance before a court. Anita Travers, in an excellent article published in *The Genealogists Magazine* (Vol. 2, No. 1, March 1983), tells us that there were more than sixty offences liable to be tried by the court leet and more

Goddard Manor Court Book Manor of Swindon 19 October 1750

than forty by the court baron. These include such things as murder, treason, rape, arson, counterfeiting and burglary, all of which were referred to the assizes. Most petty offences, like assault, bloodshed, forestalling and regrating, using false weights and measures, breaking the assizes of bread and ale, selling corrupt victuals, bawdyness, eavesdropping, gossiping, diverting or fouling highways or watercourses, failing to maintain the watch or hue and cry, (which meant rallying all available help to pursue an offender), were punishable by a fine or a period in the stocks or pillory. Other actions, such as trespass and debt, were also tried and recorded.

The manor and the parish did not always cover the same area. Often there were a number of parishes in one manor. Anita Travers, in her article, tells us that it is estimated that there were between 25,000 and 65,000 manors and 10,000 ancient parishes.

Should you require to see the existing manorial records of any county, the place to start would be the Local County Record Office. Some manorial records are still in the hands of the present Lords of the Manor. Others are scattered around in various other places.

If you are searching for manor rolls, it is worth a visit to view the Manorial Documents Register. This is a compilation of the manors, arranged in county order, which details the location of all known existing records. It is housed at The National Register of Archives, The Royal Commission on Historical Manuscripts Quality House, Quality Court, Chancery Lane, London, just further along towards High Holborn from the Public Record Office. It must be stressed they do not hold the records, only their locations.

Manorial Terms

Affeerers	Officers of the court.
Amercement	Fine paid in the manorial court.
Copyhold	Tenancy of land under the lord of the manor recorded on the official roll and a copy given to the tenant.
Custumal	Customs of the manor; services owed to the lord by tenants and obligations and rights of the lord.
Essoin	Excuse for non-attendance at manorial court or a monetary payment.
Fealty	Oath of allegiance to the Crown.
Heriot	Surrender of the best beast or dead chattel of a deceased tenant due to the lord of the manor. Sometimes a monetary payment.
Homage	Pledge of loyalty by tenants to the lord.
Homagers	Tenants who acted as a jury at manorial courts.
Messuage	A dwelling house with out-buildings and land.
Moiety	A half.

Pound/Pinfold	Enclosure for stray animals.
Quit Claim	The formal renunciation of a claim.
Seizin/Seisin	Possession of land by freehold.
Suit	Prosecution of a claim in a court of law.
Tail	A provision by which the possession of an estate is limited to a person and his heirs.
Frankpledge	A system whereby every man had to become one of a group of ten to twelve people. Each being responsible for the good behaviour of the other members. If one stepped out of line, the rest of the group could have been fined.
Waste	Uncultivated/land and within a manor.

Further reading

How to Locate and use Manorial Records by Patrick Palgrave-Moore (Elvery Dowers 1985).

The Manor and Manor Records by N.E. Hone (1925).

Life on the English Manor by H.S. Bennett (Alan Sutton Publishing 1987).

CHAPTER 11

Directories and Newspapers

Directories

Directories, mainly trade and street directories, are of tremendous help in tracing an address, especially if a forbear has been 'lost' or has moved house between the dates on birth, marriage, and death certificates from civil registration, or between dates of census returns from 1841 through to 1881 and after.

The first directory of all was one for London in 1671 which contained only names of gentry and local officials, but gradually throughout the years, directories came to include private residents, craftsmen, and other names and addresses. Often a short but invaluable history of the village, town, or city

Kelly's Directory 1839 for Tolpuddle

DIRECTORY.	2711	TOLPUDDLE. [DORSET.]

TOLPUDDLE, or Tolpiddle, a village in the Dorchester Union, Hundred of Piddletown, contained 363 inhabitants in 1841, situated about 7 miles north-east of Dorchester, and 15 south-west from Wimborne, it being on the old turnpike-road between these places. The church is a moderate-sized fabric, built of very small stone, has a tower and 4 bells; the chancel had gone to decay, but was rebuilt about 10 years since. The living is a vicarage, value £240, in the patronage of the Dean and Canons of Christ Church, Oxford. There is a small chapel, used by Wesleyans. The river Piddle bounds the village southward, and supplies a small flour-mill here.

Warren Rev. Thomas, M.A. [rector]	Bullen John, beer retailer & shopkeepr	Way Thomas, blacksmith
Brine Charles, boot & shoe maker	Bullen Wm. parish clerk & carpenter	Woodsford Wm. beer retailer & shpkpr
Brine James, miller & farmer	Smith Thomas, dairyman	Letters are left at the post office
Brine William, farmer	Way Joseph, boot & shoe maker	Piddletown

TONER'S PUDDLE, or TURNER'S PUDDLE, a parish in the Hundred of Hundred's Barrow, and Union of Wareham and Purbeck, situated about 7½ miles north-west-by-west from Wareham, and 1 mile south-west from Bere Regis. The living is a discharged rectory, a peculiar of the Dean of Salisbury, value £140, in the gift of James Frampton, Esq., of Moreton House; the present rector is the Rev. Richard Waldy, M.A. The church is an ancient structure, with nave, chancel, and square embattled tower. The parish comprises 1,930 acres. James Frampton, Esq., is lord of the manor and owner of the soil. The population, in 1841, was 122. The river Piddle runs through this parish.

Hooper John, farmer, Throop farm	Hooper William, farmer	Letters received through Bere Regis

TURNWORTH, a parish, in Blandford Union, forming with the parishes of Belchalwell and Shillingstone, a detached portion of that part of the Hundred of Cranborne, which is in the West Shaston division, being locally in the Hundred of Pimperne, 5 miles west-by-north from Blandford, contained, in 1841, 89 inhabitants. The living is a discharged vicarage, in the archdeaconry of Dorset and diocese of Salisbury, valued at £135, and in the patronage of the Bishop of Salisbury. The Rev. Thomas Tyrwhitt, M.A., is the incumbent. The church, dedicated to St. Mary, is a small edifice, with a square embattled tower. William Parry Okeden, Esq., is lord of the manor. Thorncomb is a hamlet.

Okeden William Parry, esq. Turn-	Loder Joseph, carpenter & wheelwrght	Letters are received through the
worth house	Watts William, farmer	Blandford office

TYNEHAM, or West Tyneham, a parish in the Hundred of Hasler, and Union of Wareham and Purbeck, situated about 4 miles west-by-south from Corfe Castle, and 7 south-by-west from Wareham, in the Isle of Purbeck. The living is a rectory, annexed to that of Steeple, in the diocese of Salisbury, and patronage of the Rev. Nathaniel Bond, B.A., of the Grange. The church, which is dedicated to St. Mary, is a small structure, with nave, chancel, and no tower; it was repaired in 1744. This parish is bounded on the south by the English channel, on the coast of which is a circular battery, for the defence of Warbarrow bay. Here was formerly an Alien priory, subordinate to the Abbey of Bec, in Normandy, which, at the suppression, was given by Henry VI. to St. Anthony's Hospital, London; by Edward IV. to Eton College, and afterwards to the Dean and Prebendaries of Westminster. This parish comprises about 2,840 acres, and in 1841, contained a population of 260. Tyneham House, the seat of the Rev. Wm. Bond, M.A., is a handsome and commodious mansion, most delightfully situated. Great Tyneham and South Tyneham are hamlets.

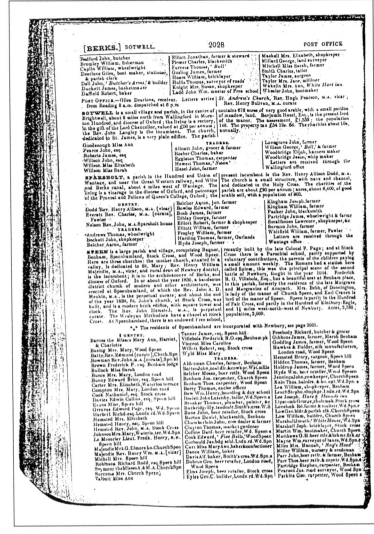

Post Office Directory — 1839

is included which should be read and noted as it will give names of charities and when they were bestowed, dates of chapels and churches, schools, public houses, posting inns, and carriers together with names and times of arrivals and departures — in fact, useful background material for a family history. Many large towns had their own directories from around 1773 but smaller places would only be catered for at intervals, often being listed in with the nearest town. Some national directories which cover various counties are those of Kelly's Post Office; Billing; White; Pigot, etc. In time, local directories came into being, mainly around the middle of the nineteenth century, giving names and addresses of householders, farmers and traders.

Directories should, at all times, be used in conjunction with civil registration certificates and census returns to find names of forbears who seem to have mysteriously disappeared! People seemed to have moved home more frequently in towns and cities than in the country — more than likely moving to larger places as the family expanded, or even doing a 'moonlight flit' when unable to pay the rent.

Telephone directories are another useful source in more ways than one. Unusual surnames can be sought to pin-point an area of 'today's families' maybe to contact to find out if they are members of 'the family'. The first telephone directory appeared in April 1880 for just over 300 London subscribers. As the telephone became a popular means of fast personal contact for business and personal reasons, so telephone directories were issued.

In my own family history, I can remember my father telling me that when he arrived home on leave during the first World War he phoned his mother to say he was in England. My grandparents were quite 'small' in trade and yet they had a telephone — the number, I remember was twenty-eight!

This particular source seems to be relatively untapped by the family historian, and yet, it, like trade directories, can be more than useful at the beginning of tracing a family history. Directories may be found in larger reference libraries, local history library collections and record offices. The largest collection for the country is in the Guildhall Library, Aldermanbury, London.

Newspapers

Newspapers are an invaluable aid to family background sources and contain news of events as they actually happened. In effect, they are historic time capsules and as such are worthy of inclusion in a research programme. Newspapers began in the seventeenth century but until the middle of the eighteenth century did not contain much in the way of personal items. From this time on they should always be looked at for local and family events in an ancestral area for an obituary, birth, marriage, death notices or business advertisements. If, for instance, a death certificate shows that an inquest took place for some reason, look at the newspaper of the area where the death occurred for an account of the inquest and maybe for events which led to the death. It is worth noting that as coroners' inquisitions are closed to the public for 75 years and even then do not always survive, a newspaper report is of importance. If there has been a divorce, bankruptcy, crime, deeds of valour, scandal, or if someone in the family has been in business or served his or her community in an official capacity, then a provincial or even a national newspaper is the source, but it is advisable to look always at more than one paper to gain a balanced view.

British, world and social history events are all within the pages of a newspaper. In 1926, at the time of the National Strike, Swindon Trade Unions published their own newspaper for a few months and this short-lived newspaper makes interesting reading for anyone who had relatives concerned with the strike in this area of Wiltshire.

One of the oldest newspapers is the *London Gazette* which, in 1666, reported on the Great Fire of London as it actually happened, but its main value lies in reports of official appointments of church, state, military personnel and bankruptcy proceedings amongst other informative announcements. The Guildhall Library in London has a complete set of this newspaper. Another important journal was the *Gentleman's Magazine* (from 1731 to 1868) which has reports similar to the *London Gazette* with lists of births, marriages, and obituaries, and complete series are to be found in the British Library, the Public Record Office, the Society of Genealogists, and some major reference libraries have partial sets and indexes. *The Times* (from 1785) newspaper indexes may be found in many libraries together with a microfilm of the newspaper from its early days.

The largest collection of newspapers in this country is to be found at the British Newspaper Library, Colindale Avenue, London, NW9 5HE. It is open from 10.00 a.m. to 4.45 p.m. Monday to Saturday and contains daily and weekly newspapers and periodicals, including London newspapers and journals, from about 1800 onwards, and English provincial, Scottish and Irish newspapers from around 1700 onwards. There are also large collections of Commonwealth and foreign newspapers.

The catalogue system provides two sets of entries, one arranged geographically by countries, counties, and towns and the other by titles of newspapers and is simple to use. Many of the newspapers are now on microfilm to prevent wear and tear on original papers. A reader's ticket is needed but this is usually provided on the spot on production of identification such as a driving licence or passport.

Some bibliographies of newspapers for certain counties have been published and it is worth enquiring to see if there is one for 'your' county. It is also advisable to take a general map of England to help when deciding just where to look for newspaper coverage of a particular area. Photocopying facilities are available at the Newspaper Library. The Burney Collection of Newspapers from 1603 to 1800 are housed in the British Library, Bloomsbury, London, as is the Thomason Collection for the Civil War and Commonwealth period. The Bodleian Library at Oxford has a collection of newspapers dating from 1622 to 1800. In the case of the British Library and the Bodleian Library, any request to use their collections must be made in writing, with your reasons for wanting to read these newspapers. Many county record offices and reference libraries hold copies of their local newspapers, often from the commencement of publication, both the original and on microfilm. The India Office Library and Records has a collection of Indian newspapers in English which is one of the finest in existence, dating from 1780, although the late nineteenth and early twentieth century ones are particularly good. This is an on-going collection. The Library has a card catalogue system with full entries under both title and place of publication. there are comprehensive collections of serials, and official gazettes published in and relating to South Asia. Photocopying facilities are available. The address is India Office Library and Records, Orbit House, 197 Blackfriars Road, London, SE1 8NG.

Further reading

A History of the London Gazette 1665-1965 (HMSO 1965).

Tercentenary Handlist of English and Welsh Newspapers 1620-1920 (The Times 1920).

The English Newspapers by Keith Williams (Springwood Books 1977).

Willings Annual Press Guide (British Media Publications).

Local Newspapers 1750-1920 by J.S.W. Gibson (FFHS 1987)

Handlist of English Provincial Newspapers and Periodicals 1700-1760 by G.A. Cranfield

Catalogue of English Newspapers and Periodicals in the Bodleian Library 1622-1800 by R.T. Milford & D.M. Sutherland (1936).

Benn's Newspaper Press Directory.

Family History from Newspapers by Eve MacLaughlin (FFHS 1987).

Guide to National and Provincial Directories of England and Wales (excluding London) before 1856 by J.E. Norton (1950).

The London Directories 1677-1855 by C.W.F. Goss (1932).

CHAPTER 12

Miscellaneous Sources

Army, Navy or Air Force ancestry

There is a tremendous amount of documentation available for those whose ancestors served in the Armed forces or the Merchant Navy. The majority of this can be found in the Public Record Office.

Very few records before 1660 exist, but for the years between then and the outbreak of the First World War, many of the documents are a positive mine of information. The outline of the story of the army life of Farrier-Major Avison, told in our introduction, will give you an idea of the valuable information to be gleaned from this source.

As with most other types of records, problems arise where runs are incomplete. In the case of army documents, many were destroyed by enemy action during World War Two. For details of records of other ranks from 1913 onwards, written application must be made to the Ministry of Defence, but this is one of the areas which suffered from German bombing. Except for the Royal Artillery, who have their own repository, the records of the officers services until1954 are with the PRO Although this is a rather specialized area of research, it should not cause too many problems, so long as you go about the task in a businesslike manner. Before starting to delve into these records we would thoroughly recommend you obtain a copy of *Tracing Your Ancestors in the Public Record Office* by Jane Cox and Timothy Padfield (HMSO 1984). This invaluable and yet reasonably priced publication may be purchased from booksellers or is generally available in most public reference libraries.

Many other lines of enquiry are available at the PRO (see Chapter 13, for a comprehensive list of their leaflets). Another useful source of information is the War Graves Commission. This most helpful organization will even send you a photograph of your ancestor's grave if he is buried in one of the cemeteries under its jurisdiction. Naturally, when approaching them it is only right to give as much correct information as possible.

A war memorial erected to men and women who died or were lost at sea during the First and Second World Wars is on the front at Southsea in Hampshire. Their names are recorded on this magnificent monument under the name of the ship and their rank. The Royal Air Force Museum, Aerodrome Road, Hendon, London also has a library which may be of use to those tracing air force ancestry during the First and Second World Wars.

Charities

From time immemorial, bequests in wills have been left for charity. The variety of charities were so numerous that it is virtually impossible to list them all — suffice it to say, that many depended on the whims and eccentricities of their donors! It was a custom for those who had money to leave a sum to be invested for the good of the parish, the church, or to assist the less well-off men, women and children in many ways.

Much of the money bequeathed was invested in stock and consuls or land to bring in an annual sum. Unfortunately in some parishes, charity affairs were mismanaged to such an extent that the bequest was often frittered away. Other parish officials managed so well that after centuries some of these charities are still in existence today.

An Act of 1812 required trustees of charities (with some exceptions) to register a memorial with the clerk of the peace. This had to include a statement of real and personal estate, gross annual income, investment, and the object of the charity, names of founders, trustees and persons in possession of the deeds of the foundation. Charity Commissioners were permanently established in 1853 to safeguard and oversee the control of existing charities.

The main type of charities were — clothing for poor men, women and children; food, for example a loaf of bread to be given to all who attended morning service on a certain Sunday in the year often with an enlightening sermon preached in memory of the benefactor; endowments for charity schools, hospitals, apprenticeships, and so on.

In a village called Thorverton, a Mary West in 1694 left a yearly rent charge of 35s. 2d. out of a house in Exeter which was to provide petticoats for poor women of the parish. In Littleham, Robert Drake in 1628 left land in trust for charitable and public uses for the relief of his poor relations! In 1778 in Georgeham, a John Richards left £5 a year to supply two school-mistresses for Georgeham and the neighbouring village of Croyde.

A Maud Heath, widow of Langley Burrell, over 500 years ago used to tramp to Chippenham market every week to sell her butter and eggs. So weary was she of the terrible road with its holes and ruts that she left all her worldly goods in 1474 to make a pavement to Chippenham. In was one of the best country pavements and still known to this day as Maud Heath's Causeway. A statue was erected in 1698, and Maud in her bonnet with stick and basket sat on a high stone column, which was inscribed with the words 'Injure me not' on one side and a sundial on the other side.

One day during research, a letter was found concerning a great-grandmother who had been given ten shillings in 1859 from a charity bequeathed by a Miss Elizabeth Benet in 1743 who left £200 to be invested in land which was to bring about £7 yearly to be given to poor girls upon entering domestic service to buy a new frock. The letter was worded:-

> Mr Watts,
> Sir,
>   I beg to inform you that we have a girl liveing with us name
> Mary Collier Daughter of John Collier She have no Mother She
> have been liveing with us Severel years She is a very good girl
> and I think She is Deserveing the Chariety money if you would
> be kind enough to give it to her it will will be Thankfily received
> by her.
>
>   from your most huble Se[nt]
>   D. Cowley.

On further investigation, D. Cowley turned out to be Mary Collier's uncle,
David, a baker in the village of Wroughton, with whom she had gone to live
when she was 7 years old on the death of her mother. A delightful little cameo
for a family history.

   Often, in the parish registers or churchwardens' accounts will be found items
known as 'briefs' and these were collections taken, usually after divine service
on a Sunday, for disasters which had occurred throughout the country, such
as a fire or flood which had destroyed much of a town or village, and in many
cases some of the inhabitants. There were also collections for those in captivity
and prisoners of the Turks. Apparently, these collections came in such rapid
succession that many parishioners obviously tired of doling out their hard-
earned pennies for places and people of whom they had never heard that
sometimes only a few pennies would be collected.

Deeds

The Statute of Enrolments in 1535/6 stated that no transfer of land was to
take place unless the indenture was sealed and enrolled with the Clerk of
the Peace of a county. This gave rise to a general series of enrolled deeds
of bargain and sale including awards under the Inclosure Act from 1733 (see
Chapter 7 — Quarter Sessions). Of course, some counties are better served
than others in the amount of deeds contained in the county record office,
even so, this source should always be consulted when tracing ancestral homes
and family relationships.

   During the early eighteenth century an attempt was made to set up local
deed registries but, unfortunately it did not come to fruition except for four
areas:

East Riding Registry of Deeds, Humberside County Hall, Beverley, North
Humberside HO17 9BA.

North Riding Registry of Deeds, North Yorkshire Record Office, County Hall,
Northallerton, N. Yorks, DL7 8SG.

Registry of Deeds, West Yorkshire Record Office, Newstead Road, Wakefield,
W. Yorks, WF1 2DE.

Middlesex Registry of Deeds, Greater London Record Office, 40 Northampton
Road, London, EC1R 0HB.

There are Registries of Deeds for Ireland and Scotland:

Registry of Deeds, Henrietta Street, Dublin.
Scottish Record Office, HM Register House, Princes Street, Edinburgh, EH1 3YY.

Divorce

In the days when this country was wholly Roman Catholic the ecclesiastical courts dealt with matters relating to marriage and its dissolution with a right of appeal to the Pope. This state of affairs continued until the reign of Henry VIII with the Act of Supremacy and the Statute of Appeals, when the Crown became the supreme authority in all matters appertaining to the Church, and the right of appeal to Rome was abolished.

After the Reformation church courts dealt with all business concerning annulment, separation, and divorce and this continued up to the eighteenth century when divorce was only achieved by a Private Act of Parliament passed in the House of Lords. Between 1715 and 1852 about 240 dissolutions were recorded. Before this period the church courts could authorize a legal separation which was called a divorce or 'mensa et thoro' which, literally translated meant 'from table and bed'. Both parties, however, had to promise not to re-marry during the lifetime of the other partner. On the other hand, a marriage could be dissolved on the grounds of pre-contract — 'ab initio', meaning 'from the beginning' but this procedure, which was not uncommon, was abolished in 1754. Records of these separations and divorces which took place in the church courts are to be found in diocesan archives either in a diocesan record office or in a county record office.

Many husbands and wives who wanted a legal separation would not necessarily attend their local church court but would often journey to London to the Consistory Court there. The first civil court to be given power of dissolution was the Court for Divorce and Matrimonial Causes set up following the 1857 Matrimonial Causes Act which allowed for divorce on grounds of adultery by the wife and various 'offences' by the husband; it also included cruelty as a reason for dissolution in a petition by the wife. The grounds for divorce remained much the same right up to 1937.

From 1858 until 1937 divorce records are kept at the Public Record Office, Chancery Lane, London, under the records of the Supreme Court of Judicature, classified under the group J 77 and J 78. Files are closed to the public for 100 years but the indexes to them are open for inspection. Permission to look at the papers of an individual case may be obtained from the Principal Registry of the Family Division, Somerset House, Strand, London. For divorce after 1937 application should also be made to the Family Division, Somerset House.

One solution to the problem of finding more information about a specific divorce case where files are closed because of the 100 year old rule is to look at newspapers of the time and area where the case was heard as well as local papers of the couple's home town. It is advisable to look at more than one newspaper to gain an overall report. Of course, couples who wanted to separate or who wanted to live with someone else did not always resort to church or civil courts and would often decide to go their own ways, occasionally 'bigamously' marrying another partner until the law caught up with them or they would just decide to live together without the sanctity of marriage, or a divorce.

Enclosures

Until the eighteenth century most of the land in England was cultivated on the 'open field' system which was generally on the principal of three arable fields, one of which was laid down with crops for the winter, the second to be sown in the spring and the third would be left to lie fallow. A farmer or tenant would hold a number of strips in each field, but there could be no variety in the crops, as each strip in the field had to be sown with the same crop and cultivated and harvested at the same time by the men who were responsible for their particular strips. In addition, each strip had to be separated by a small earthen bank giving a network of footpaths to enable a man to have access to his strips without encroaching on his neighbour's plot.

Obviously, this system was not economical, as men would quarrel, one would weed and cultivate and another would not. Eventually, throughout England, the system of enclosing the land by hedges and ditches took place, this meant also the division and take-over of the common land, where the poorest man and woman had been able, from time immemorial, to sow a few crops and graze their animals. Even their ancient rights to wood and wasteland disappeared under this system of enclosure, which brought about untold misery and privation to many labourers and their families, almost to the point of starvation. Some counties in England, such as Essex, Surrey, Devon, and parts of the Midlands, had been enclosed during Tudor times, but over a large part of central and northern England the method of 'open-field' farming was still in existence in the eighteenth century.

The revolution in farming methods by such men as Jethro Tull, Thomas Coke and Viscount Townshend who had introduced new crops and farming procedures into the country, as well as the fact that enclosure of the fields and commons benefited above all the wealthy landowner, seemed to speed up the enclosures. From 1760 to 1797 some 15,000 private enclosure acts were passed through Parliament. In 1801 a General Enclosure Act was passed which did away with the need for private enclosure acts, and in 1836 another Enclosure Act was passed which authorized enclosure of the fields if two-thirds of the interested parties were in agreement. By 1854 yet another Enclosure Act gave Commissioners the right to consider any applications and they were also authorized to allocate some land for exercise and recreation. At long last the enclosures were complete and were eventually brought to an end by the Curtailment of Enclosures Act in 1876.

Our ancestors during these last hundred years had seen a tremendous change in the countryside, a change reflected in their lives and social conditions. One or two open fields with their strips still exist today and have been preserved for posterity, such as the great 'open-fields' at Braunton in North Devon, and Laxton, Nottinghamshire.

As a result of the various acts, maps of enclosures, and the awards which accompany them, should be found in the records of the Clerk of the Peace in county record offices, although at times they may be discovered hidden away in parish collections. The PRO at Kew also has some awards. Documentation about the early Tudor enclosures may be discovered in county record offices or in the PRO, Chancery Lane collections, such as the Exchequer, State Papers Domestic and Chancery but, unfortunately, these are comparatively rare and somewhat difficult to find.

Maps

Family historians rely on maps of all types, from those especially designed for the purpose of research which cover all parishes and will jurisdictions with dates of commencement of parish registers for each county in Great Britain, to ordnance survey maps from around 1805 up to the present day.

Map of Swindon by Orlando Baker. Found in the North Wilts Directory of 1883 (Old & New Swindon)

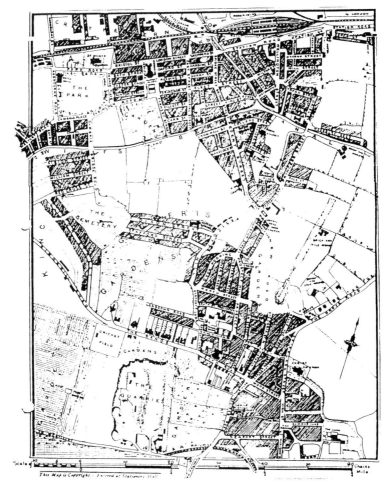

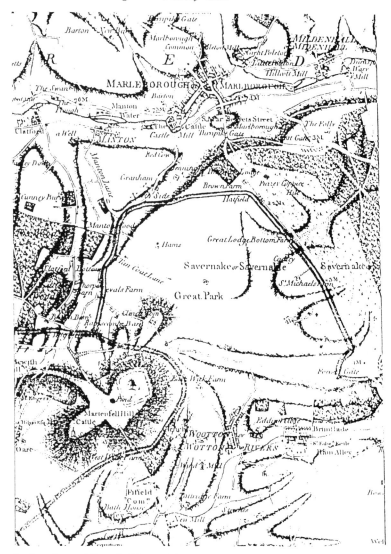

Andrew's and Dury's Map of Wiltshire 1773 — Marlborough

Maps date back to very early days and some of these are of value as a genealogist's research goes back in time, such as Camden's 1607 Britannia county maps; John Speed's county maps with the county town, and John Ogilby's Britannia series of road or coaching maps.

County record offices and reference libraries usually hold extensive series of maps for their own area ranging from railway, canal, estate and manorial survey maps to town and city maps of varying dates. Many family and estate records deposited in county record offices contain private maps of their holdings. Two of the principal types of maps that need to be looked at are the ones known as tithe and enclosure maps both accompanied by awards giving names, acreage and rent. Tithe maps and awards have been dealt with more fully in Chapter 7.

When researching in a record office or library it is wise to include in your 'homework' file an ordnance survey map of 'your area' together with a parish map so that it can be easily seen what parish to search next or where someone may have moved to live and work. Take a 1″ scale map with family parishes and areas marked with a highlight pen so that the spread of family ancestry can be seen at a glance; this with a county parish map similarly marked helps considerably during research when the question arises — as it inevitably does — where to search next? Finally, maps may be used in conjunction with the series of 'Place Name' books. These books give variations of place names from the earliest known to the present day spelling.

The map illustrated is of Swindon, Wiltshire dated 1883 by Orlando Baker and was found in a trade directory. It shows the division between the ancient parish of Swindon, on the hill, and the new Swindon which had grown up around the Great Western Railway, at that stage of its growth before the making of the borough in 1900 which combined the old and new Swindon. This map can be used to pin-point streets with the 1881 census return and for registration certificates of births, marriages and deaths of Swindon people at this time.

The 1773 map is a typical example of a county map of the period.

'Members' interests' and genealogical directories

All family history societies publish what are known as 'members' interests' in their journals. That is to say, members supply the surnames which they are researching together with the areas and approximate dates. In this way, members may contact others working on the same name and very often establish long lost relationships. Some, not all, societies publish directories of the members' interests which may be purchased, and *Family Tree Magazine* publishes a list of readers' interests each month. In this way, family historians all over the world can see if anyone else is working on 'their name'.

As well as 'members' interests' other books called 'genealogical directories' are published on a subscriber basis. Two of the better known ones are the series of National Genealogical Directories from 1979 formerly edited by Michael Burchall of Brighton and the Genealogical Research Directory (GRD) — a key reference work for worldwide family history research edited by Keith A. Johnson and Malcolm R. Sainty published yearly since 1982. Everyone who contributes their surnames on a subscriber basis receives a free copy of the next directory which contains their entries of surnames being researched. The aim, as with 'members' interests', is to put family historians in touch with one another and so avoid duplication of research. The directories contain subscribers names and addresses in a list with a number in numerical order by the side. This is 'their' number which appears by the side of the surnames they have contributed. When using the directories, looking through to find who else may be researching your surname in your ancestral area, the number given there is the one you need to find the name and address of that person. Do remember when writing to anyone to include a S.A.E. and keep your first letter to specific and concise details. Many of these directories and published family history societies members' interests are to be found in major public reference libraries under the genealogical section, libraries of family history societies for the use of their members, and in genealogical societies, where they may also be on sale.

Missing relatives
The Department of Health and Social Security (DHSS)
Whilst in the first stages of beginning your family history you may decide you would like to contact a relative, perhaps an elderly aunt, uncle, or a cousin and then you suddenly realize you have no idea of their present address. It is possible to contact that relative through the medium of the Department of Health and Social Security.

The Department will not disclose an address but are quite happy to send on a stamped sealed letter to the last known address shown on their records, if the information you supply with your letter is sufficient for them to identify that person. You need to send the person's full name, last known address, last known marital status, and age or approximate age.

If, however, they have sent on your letter to your relation and you have not received a reply it may be that she or he does not want to reply or, as is often the case, they keep on putting off the task until 'tomorrow'. The next step is then, perhaps, make a journey to the last known address and see if the person is still living there, or contact one of the neighbours who may be able to help you further. The DHSS address is:

The Department of Health and Social Security, Special Section 'A', Records 'B', Newcastle upon Tyne, NE98 1YU.

Do not forget to include a stamped addressed envelope in with your sealed letter for your relative to reply. Of course, your relative may have died and to satisfy yourself that you have made every effort, you could search the death indexes at St. Catherine's House.

Another method is to write to the local newspaper asking for anyone who knows that person or their whereabouts to contact you, and it does help to say that you are tracing your family history.

Monumental inscriptions (MI)
Gravestones mark burial places of our ancestors and it is the information on these stones, known as monumental inscriptions, or MIs for short, that help identify relationships with dates and places. They are a source which will help prove ancestry and may give new leads where necessary. For example, not only can an MI give details of a man, his wife, and children but, at times, more information, as to birth places, a second marriage, or a place of residence.

Not all gravestones necessarily mark a burial place, however, but may be memorials to those who have died in some distant place where they have been buried. In the 1800s when this country was empire-building, many British men and women lived and served abroad in various capacities and their deaths may be remembered on a stone back in their home parish churchyard.

Most Family History Societies have a county-wide project to record their church monumental inscriptions, wherever they may be, in churchyards, churches, non-conformist burial grounds, cemeteries. In addition, any inscriptions appearing on memorial windows, plaques, memorial books and war cenotaphs are recorded. Therefore, it is always worthwhile contacting a county family history society to find whether they have listed the MIs for the area in which you are interested before going to see if a gravestone marks the actual burial place of a forbear. It must be noted that not all burials are marked with a gravestone and monumental inscription and that in some cases the ravages of time may have made them unreadable.

More and more churchyards are now being cleared of gravestones, and the ground levelled and landscaped. Often only a small notice of intent appears in the local newspaper, hidden away in an obscure corner. If family historians are interested in preserving records for posterity they can either obtain permission from the authority concerned and record the inscriptions themselves or contact the local family history society through their public reference library who will be able to supply the secretary's name and address. The secretary will then get in touch with members of the society, who will record the inscriptions before the stones are taken away and disposed of, and vital records will be preserved.

A Baptist chapel in Swindon was due to be converted into a dwelling house; the chapel yard levelled and the stones disposed of. A solicitor who had inserted the notice in the local newspaper was quickly contacted and permission obtained to record inscriptions. The solicitor said his clerk had already recorded as many of them as he could read but most of these turned out to be incorrect. After half a day's work, the inscriptions were recorded, with copies going to the solicitor, the local family history society, and the Society of Genealogists. In this case, luckily, details were taken just in time.

Projects and indexes

Many organizations, societies, and individuals keep and maintain indexes of all kinds. Some people prefer to work completely on their own transcribing and indexing a variety of records and archives. Others work in groups on larger projects. For instance, family history societies collect and index such items as monumental inscriptions for their counties as well as non-conformist registers, census returns, and parish registers. Some transcribe and index marriages or baptisms for a certain area. Transcriptions and indexes are made by responsible and interested people who endeavour to put something back into their hobby for the advantage of other historians in their research as well as preserving original books and documents and so save wear and tear on unique records. Of course, all indexes and transcriptions must be treated as 'finding aids' only and must be used as a lead back to the original source to check all is correct.

Record societies transcribe historical records and parish registers for their own area or county and put them into print. These books should be found in county record offices, local history collections and reference libraries.

Enquiries should be made about such reference books for an ancestral area. If ancestry has been well established in a certain county then it may well be worthwhile to join such a record society to receive their yearly printings.

It is only possible to list here a few of the variety of indexes which are available:

> Apprenticeships.
> Coastguards.
> Chancery proceedings such as the Bernau Index in the Society of Genealogist's Library.
> Emigrants and Immigrants.
> Boyd's Marriage Index which covers parts of various counties to 1837.
> Transported persons.
> Prisoners of War.
> Canal, River boats and boatmen.
> Trades and tradesmen.
> Settlements, Removals and Examinations.
> Wills and Administrations.
> London and other Prisons from the 1851 Census.

One important index is the Federation of Family History Society's 'Strays Index' which covers all births, baptisms, marriages, deaths, and burials which occur in another county or country, and not in a person's normal place of abode. All members of family history societies are encouraged to gather up all strays found during the course of their own research and send them in to the Strays co-ordinator for their region. It is surprising just how many 'lost' ancestors may be found in this way.

It must be pointed out that there is usually a small charge made by the person maintaining an index to cover running costs.

Schools

School registers, log books and admission records are of value, not only for helping to establish ancestry but also to provide information about our forbears which may not be found elsewhere. If research has taken you into the professional classes, such as lawyers, clergy, and gentry, then look at public school records and those of universities. Many of the records for the well-known public schools are in print, as are those of Oxford and Cambridge Universities.

As for the 'ordinary' people who make up the rest of the population, there were a variety of schools which provided an education of some sort, but it must be realized that until the Education Act of 1879/80, when schooling for all children up to 10 years of age was made compulsory, the majority of our ancestors did not receive any kind of an education and were never able to read and write at all.

There were a variety of schools provided for the education of children, for example charity schools, dame schools and ragged schools. Records of these are mainly found in county record offices. Records of schools under the control of local education authorities should be still at the school or in county record offices.

The printed word

Various books have been recommended as further reading at the end of each chapter of this book and an extensive bibliography has also been included. These are the printed sources which will assist research into your family history. There comes a time when research seems to be reasonably complete, although the feeling persists that just around the corner some great find or break-through is about to happen! A decision has to be made at some point to call a halt in order to write up in one form or another all the finds you have discovered during the long hours of work you have done and, at last, put pen to paper and start writing the family history for yourself, relatives, and future descendants. It is at this time, more than ever before, that the 'printed word' needs to be utilized to set your family into the every day social and historical picture of its life and times.

Every county has books on all aspects of its history and topography, some well-known and some not so well-known, but all valuable in their own way to help 'put flesh on the bare bones'. Some counties have bibliographies of all books to do with their area and these are more than useful to refer to. It is also wise to refer to the bibliography of any book which you read in connection with genealogy as this leads to more sources.

General works such as the following examples refer, generally, to all counties, some are more comprehensive than others. The series of Victoria County Histories, or VCH as they are known, appear for most counties, although some counties are not so widely covered as others. The VCH give detailed histories of a county from its beginnings through to the present day. Histories of parishes are given from their origins to their manors, churches, non-conformist chapels, schools, trades, and people of note who helped develop and form the village or town.

Another series are the county Notes and Queries, again, some are more extensive than others. These books and others similar help to fill in family background with information not to be found elsewhere, as we have found ourselves with our own family histories, providing folklore, superstitions, historical notes, and so on for ancestral counties and parishes. Many counties, cities and some towns have their own Record Societies and publications and these should never be overlooked or discounted, similarly all the various local history society publications for your area. It is well-known that local historians have a deep and extensive knowledge of their own village, town, or city and it is wise to seek out this type of history.

In the nineteenth century there appeared printed volumes of transcribed marriages for certain parishes for nearly every county, usually up to 1812 or a little beyond, known as *Phillimore's Marriages* and these are yet another source which are to be found in a county record office or reference library. And so, the list goes on... For years now, ever since first starting family history I have tried to collect, wherever possible, all books and literature to do with 'my county' as well as the county in which I live. Obviously, I have not been able to afford all I would have liked but it is surprising how many turn up in second hand shops and in library sales at quite a nominal sum. Those I have been unable to afford or obtain because of rarity or cost have been ordered through the inter-loan library system at the local public library for a few pence, to borrow and return. Gradually, in this way, I have built up my knowledge and understanding of my 'ancestral' county together with the usual historical and social volumes of English and world history.

Other sources for the more advanced researcher

Besides the well trodden path of civil or parish records there is a seemingly endless variety of other sources of information. These records were created, for one reason or another totally unconnected with genealogy, and contain many names and addresses. Many can prove to be positive goldmines of information. Here are a few of the more useful:-

Merchant Seamen

A surprising number of our ancestors, at some time or other in their lifetimes, spent time as merchant seamen. Many records of these are available for viewing at the Public Record Office at Kew. For more information see *My Ancestor was a Merchant Seaman* by C.T. and M.J. Watts (Society of Genealogists).

Passports

Although passports were not made compulsory until 1914 they were in use by many travellers dating from 1795. The register is available at the Public Record Office in the Foreign Office collection, (FO 610). During the seventeenth century there was an early form of passport issued called 'Licences to Pass Beyond the Seas' which can be of help in tracing an ancestor who travelled abroad on business. These are in the Exchequer collection at the Public Record Office, Chancery Lane.

Freemasons

The origins of freemasonry as it is known today commenced during the late seventeenth and early eighteenth centuries in this country. If an ancestor is thought to have been a member of a freemason's lodge, details of his date of entry and the name of the lodge may be obtained from The Secretary, The United Grand Lodge of England, Great Queen Street, London, WC2B 5A2 (see also Chapter 7, Records of the Clerk of the Peace).

Chartered Companies

Many of our ancestors were involved in the activities of companies such as the East India Company, the Levant Company or the Hudson Bay Company. Records of many of these have survived and give much valuable information to the researcher. The records of the Levant Company are in the Public Record

Office and the Hudson Bay Company in Canada, although records are on film at the Public Record Office, Kew. East India Company records may be seen on film at The India Office Library (see Chapter 14).

Emigrants

Much information on people who left the shores of Britain may be gained from the records at the Public Record Office: The reasons for ancestors leaving were many and varied. Vast numbers of people from Ireland emigrated to the USA at the time of the potato famine. Many others were sent to Australia as convicts. Some just felt they could create a better life for their families in another country. Many did not settle and eventually returned home and when this happened it created a large gap in the life story of an ancestor, particularly if the researcher is unaware of what happened. It may be that a couple married and went to Australia or New Zealand where they may have had two or three children and then returned to Britain This is puzzling to a modern researcher for he finds three children but is unable to determine where they were born. Census returns are invaluable for solving this problem as well as other records which are available in the Public Record Office.

Foundlings

Years ago many babies were born either out of wedlock or to parents who were unable to afford to feed another mouth. One way to remove the problem was to leave the baby in a church porch or some such similar place where it would be easily found, hence the term 'foundlings'. This was most prevalent in London. The babies were usually taken in by foundling hospitals and were often named after the place where they were found. If one such baby, for instance, was left in the porch of St. Patrick's Church, he may perhaps, be christened Patrick Church, whereas George Christmas may have been found on the steps near St. George's Church on Christmas Day. Here are some extracts to be found in the Sonning burial register in Berkshire, referring to the foundling hospital there.

1757 Ann Underwood an infant from the Foundling Hospital.
1758 Dorinda Roak: Robert Kirk: Conrade Nelson: Samuel Pope.
1759 Thomas, a child: Sophia Weston: Robert Romney.

Researchers who manage to find an ancestor who was a foundling may come across such things as apprenticeship indentures concerning the child as he or she grew older but they would, however, be very lucky indeed to find the natural parents of such a child.

Tontines

Tontines were a way in which governments raised money between 1693 and 1789. The idea proved most popular with the wealthy and the system worked thus — a person invested a sum of money and was guaranteed a yearly income during the lifetime of the person he had chosen as a partner in the scheme. For obvious reasons a younger relative was usually nominated. As the nominees died there was more money in the fund to go around fewer people and as time elapsed the annuity was worth more. Around 15,000 people joined in eleven tontines and records of these are held in the Public Record Office at Kew.

Lay Subsidies
These are records of taxes levied on the population at times when the country and the monarch was in need of money. They were usually taxes on land, goods and wages with only the very poor being exempt. Many of these have been printed for various counties. They are in the Public Record Office at Chancery Lane in the Exchequer series and exist to the end of the seventeenth century.

Muster Rolls
Men were needed for defence in times of war and muster rolls show how many men were available in a county for this purpose. Men, horses and equipment are recorded under their parish of residence. They exist to around the time of the Civil War in England and are invaluable for tracing a family before parish registers commenced. The early rolls are in the Exchequer series and later ones in State Papers at the Public Record Office, Chancery Lane.

Close Rolls
These relate to property and record some thousands of deeds of sale . So called 'Close Rolls' because each roll as it was copied was sewn on to the end of the previous roll and rolled up with the writing on the inside. Close rolls commence around 1200 and exist up to the nineteenth century. Obviously, the later ones, which are indexed, are easier to read. (Public Record Office).

Inquisitions Post Mortem
Also known as I.P.Ms. Inquisitions were held to enquire into what land a person owned at his death, thus establishing his heir, giving relationships, and property held. They are in existence from 1235 to 1650 for all counties and many have been printed. They only refer to tenants in chief of the Crown but valuable information may be gained from this source. (Public Record Office).

Feet of Fines
This unusual name comes from the fact that only the 'foot' of each fine was preserved by the Exchequer, with the other two parts being divided between the contracting parties to a change of ownership or record to title of land. (Public Record Office). Often in print. In existence to around the middle nineteenth century.

Heraldry and coats of arms
During research in parish registers, wills, and various other archives, some family historians may discover their ancestor bore a coat of arms. For many, the first finds will be through female lines, and when found this subject makes another intriguing line of work into an entirely different aspect of genealogy.

From 1529 until the late seventeenth century, enquiries were made by heralds under the authority of a commission from the Crown throughout the country to examine claims of gentlemen as to whether they were entitled to use a coat of arms — these enquiries were known as 'visitations'. At first all the principal gentry were visited by the heralds, but eventually all those desiring to claim arms or gentility were summoned to appear before the visiting herald at certain towns within a county. Their claims were examined with due regard to records of previous visitations, family records, tradition and pedigree, and so on. If a coat of arms was granted it was recorded and kept at the College of Arms. Likewise, if a claim was refused, or the person summoned did not appear it was published as having been disclaimed.

The records of visitations have been printed for most counties by the Harleian Society, and some have been published by other eminent scholars on the subject; these are known as Visitations for Devon, or Surrey, of Gloucestershire, etc. In these volumes are usually printed the disclaimers as well, under the title of 'Lists of persons disclaimed', often with the word 'ignoblis' attached. There are other publications by this society listing those who have received grants of arms between 1687 and 1898.

If, therefore, a reference is found in early parish registers, a will, or other archives, to an ancestor who is termed as 'gent', 'esquire', 'Mr' or in the case of a female 'Mrs', then it is worth looking into the possibility there may be a pedigree in one of the Harleian Society publications for that family. Obviously, as in all research, if a pedigree is discovered it must be checked, as errors and discrepancies may still be found even in such notable archives as these. Many interesting articles on the subject of heraldry, visitations, and coats of arms, may be found in the magazines of the Society of Genealogists, the Institute of Heraldic and Genealogical Studies and the Heraldry Society.

Old handwriting (paleography)

One aspect of family history which every researcher encounters is that of reading and deciphering old handwriting in parish registers, bishops transcripts, wills, and other archives. It is wise, therefore, to concentrate on learning how to read the various kinds of handwriting from the Victorian hand back through the years to the Tudor period. The main script to be found is the writing known as Secretary hand which was that usually used in parish registers in the early days, other scripts used were Court Hand and Italic Hand.

Some registers and documents may be written in Latin, except for the period of the Commonwealth from 1653 to 1660 when they were ordered to be written in English. By 1733 the law ordered all official documents were to be written in English and not Latin although in many cases Latin had been abandoned long before this date and English used instead. With practice, everyone should be able to read the ordinary hand of the parish clerk during the sixteenth and seventeenth centuries, but it must be stressed that spelling was not uniform and the same word could be spelt in a variety of ways throughout a document — this continued to the late nineteenth century when schooling was made compulsory for all.

Many of our ancestors, indeed the majority of them, were unable to read or write, and the parish clerk when writing a name in the parish registers could spell it phonetically or how it sounded to him at the time. Dialect also must be taken into consideration at all times. These differences in spelling have been explained in Chapter 4 under the heading of 'variants'. A parish register may show such an example of variation in spelling:

> *Married* 1636/7 February 20 George Rudall and Sarah Willsone
> *Baptism* 1637 December 1 Henery son of Gorge Ruddle and Sara his wife
> *Burial* 1638 March 26 Henry son of George Ridall
> *Baptism* 1640 June 4 Marie daughter of George and Sarah Rudell
> *Burial* 1641 Dec 3 Mary daughter of George Ruddle
> *Baptism* 1641 Dec 30 Mary daughter of George and Sarey Redall
> *Burial* 1641 Dec 31 Sarah wife of Geo: Rudal in childbirth.

Perseverance is needed, but most people are able to cope quite adequately after some practice in deciphering these old hands. Several books have been written on old handwriting and simple Latin with the family historian in mind, and it is helpful to include one or two of these as practical aids which can be kept in the research file on visits to record offices and libraries. Archivists are generally only too happy to help with the occasional word which cannot be read and most family history societies have one or two experts who are willing to help interpret some difficult words and phrases. It might be considered worthwhile to attend a class on how to read and interpret old handwriting, and some family history societies and genealogical societies hold the occasional day or evening class for members.

Further reading

Tracing your Ancestors in the Public Record Office by Cox & Padfield (HMSO 1984).

World War I Army Ancestry by Norman Holding (FFHS 1982).

More Sources on World War 1 Army Ancestry by Norman Holding (FFHS 1987).

Location of British Army Records by Norman Holding (FFHS 1987).

In Search of Army Ancestry by G. Hamilton-Edwards (Phillimore 1977).

A Domesday of English Enclosure Acts and Awards by W.E. Tate, ed. M.E. Turner (1978).

Common Fields and Enclosures in England 1450 to 1850 by J.A. Yelling (1977).

Common Land and Inclosure by E.C.K. Gonner (1966).

Tudor Enclosures by Joan Thirsk (Historical Assoc. 1958).

The Phillimore Atlas and Index of Parish Registers Ed. by C.R. Humphery-Smith (Phillimore).

British History Atlas by Martin Gilbert (Weidenfeld & Nicolson 1968).

Looking at Old Maps by John Booth (Cambridge House Books. Shaftesbury, Dorset. 1979).

Series of *Bartholomew's Gazetteer of Great Britain*.

Marriage, Census and Other Indexes for Family Historians ed. Jeremy Gibson (FFHS).

Bishops Transcripts and Marriage Licences, Bonds and Allegations — A guide to their location and indexes Compiled by J.S.W. Gibson (FFHS).

The Family Historians' Enquire Within by Pauline Saul and Fred Markwell (FFHS 1986).

Unpublished Personal Name Indexes in Record Offices and Libraries Compiled by J.S.W. Gibson (FFHS 1987.).

Local Historians Encyclopedia by John Richardson (Historical Publications 1986).

A Guide to the Records of the British State Tontines and Life Annuities of the 17th and 18th centuries by Francis Leeson (Pinhorns 1968).

A New Dictionary of Heraldry by Stephen Friar (Alpha Books 1987).

Heraldry Can Be Fun by J.S. Swinnerton (BMSGH 1986).

Visitation Pedigrees and the Genealogist by G.D. Squibb (2nd ed. Pinhorns London, 1978).

The Records and Collections of the College of Arms by A.R. Wagner (Burke London, 1952).

Disclaimers at the Heralds' Visitations by J.P. Rylands (Billing 1888).

Simple Heraldry by Sir Iain Moncrieffe of that Ilk (1953).

A Complete Guide to Heraldry by A.C. Fox-Davies (1961).

The Right to Arms — leaflet published by the Society of Genealogists.

A Secretary hand ABC by Alf Ison (Berkshire Family History Society 1985).

Reading Old Handwriting by Eve McLaughlin (FFHS 1987).

Simple Latin for Family Historians by Eve McLaughlin (FFHS 1986).

Examples of Handwriting 1550-1650 compiled by W.S.B. Buck (Society of Genealogists 1965).

Examples of English Handwriting 1150-1750 by Hilda E.P. Grieve (Essex Record Office Publications. 5th impression 1981).

Genealogical Research in England and Wales by Smith and Gardner. Volume 3. (Bookcraft, Salt Lake City, Utah. 1966)

A Glossary of Household, Farming and Trade Terms from Probate Inventories by Rosemary Milward (Derbyshire Record Society 1982).

Old Title Deeds by N.W. Alcock (Phillimore 1986).

CHAPTER 13

The Public Record Office (PRO)

The Public Record Office,
Chancery Lane,
London, WC2A 1LR.

The Public Record Office,
Ruskin Avenue,
Kew, Richmond,
Surrey, TW9 4DU.

Census Room of the Public Record Office,
Land Registry Building,
Portugal Street,
London, WC2A 3HP.

Opening hours are from 9.30 a.m. to 4.50 p.m. Monday to Friday, except for public holidays and the first two weeks in October when the office is closed for stocktaking. A reader's ticket is needed for admission to the search rooms but not for the Census room. The ticket will be issued on proof of identity such as a driving licence or passport. There are no car parking facilities at Chancery lane but a large car park is provided for readers at Kew. The usual rules apply as for any other record office — no food or drink in the search rooms, no smoking, sweets, or chewing gum. No children or pets. Pencils only and quietness at all times as others are working as well as you.

The Public Record Office was established in 1838 by Act of Parliament and most of the national records of government and the central law courts which, at this time, were housed in various buildings were to be brought together under one roof. The office in Chancery Lane was opened in 1856 and as the collection grew, other buildings became necessary to store documents, such as the office at Hayes in Middlesex, which is still used as an intermediate repository or records centre by fifty-four departments. Another office was opened at Kew in 1977 for what are loosely termed 'modern' records from about 1800 onwards although some of these records do date back to the

Entrance to Public Record Office, Chancery Lane, London

seventeenth century. The records at Kew are the ones of government departments and the armed services and other organizational deposits. It must be noted at this point that parliamentary records, local government and private collections will not be found in the Public Record Office. Neither are those of the Quarter Sessions which are deposited in local county record offices (see Chapter 7), although records of the Assize circuits are all in the PRO East India Company and other Indian archives are at the India Office Library and Records, 197 Blackfriars Road, London, SE1 8NG.

All the records in the Public Record Office in Chancery Lane and Kew are catalogued under Group letters, for example:-

W.O. War Office which contains army records.

ADM. Admiralty for Royal Navy records.

E. Exchequer.

I.R. Board of Inland Revenue.

Most records have a rule of 30 years before they may be seen, and certain classes such as the census returns and other secret documents have 100 year and 50 year rules.

Chancery Lane

Records in this branch of the Public Record Office are those of the law courts from the earliest times to the present day and of central government until around 1800. A sample of some of these records with their group letters are:-

Chancery (C)
Exchequer (E)
Central Criminal Court (CRIM)
Clerks of Assize (ASSI)
Prerogative Court of Canterbury (PROB)
Inland Revenue (IR)
Non-Parochial registers and records (RG)
Census Returns (HO) (RG)

Kew

Records in Kew contain modern departments of government and the armed services from about 1800. A few of these are as follows:-

Foreign Office (FO)
Colonial Office (CO)
Board of Transport (BT)
Home Office (HO)
War Office (WO)

Before undertaking research in the Public Record Office, with its wealth of information, the general step-by-step work of tracing a family history should have been largely completed. From this basic work details of the family will have been discovered and it is then known what form future research will take. Before contemplating a journey to the Public Record Office, familiarize yourself with its records by reading books and doing some homework on the types of records needed on arrival there. Obviously a first visit will be mainly one of reconnaissance to get to know the system and layout of the offices with the cataloguing system and method of ordering.

The Public Record Office issues useful and helpful leaflets and publishes booklets on many of the archives in its collection and any needed on a specific subject such as army ancestry, merchant navy, Royal Navy, immigrants, or non-conformist ancestry before 1840 etc., are obtainable either at Chancery Lane or Kew.

The Hearth Tax, where it survives, shows the number of hearths for which each household was charged at 2/- payable on Ladyday and Michaelmas. The hearths not chargeable were for those householders who were poor or if their house was not worth more than 20/- per annum.

The example opposite, typical of the Hearth Tax, is to be found in the Public Record Office at Chancery Lane and is an example of the type of record to seek in an endeavour to find more about a family and how they lived, and

Examples

Exchequer		Hearth Tax for 1664		Chancery Lane
Braunton, Devon				
John Hancock Esq.	8	Nicholas Nutt	3	
Mr John Newell	6	William Parminter	3	
Humphry Reed	2	John Peake	2	
Richard Lerwell senr.	4	.... Beare	2	
Richard Lerwell junr.	3	Thomas Challacombe	.	
Mary Norman	2	....		.
Nicholas Morrice	2			
Susan Ley	9			
Hearths not chargeable				
Richard Reade	1	William Fleming	1	
John Johns	1	Richard Barnes	1	
Katherine Phillips	1	David Hill	1	
Jesper Smith	1	Aulexander Hill	1	
Julian Rooke	1	Elizabeth Tucker	1	
John Cutley	1			

PRO Ref. E 179

Apprenticeship Registers 1710 to 1760 Inland Revenue (IR)
Selected entries for Wiltshire
Abethell alias Biffen, James son of Thomas, yeoman, of Upavon: to Elizabeth Ishare, spinster of North Bradley. 3 August 1713. £8.

Alexander Sarah: to Jane David, mantua maker, of Marden: 30 August 1756. £6.

Carpenter John son of Richard, of St. Thomas in Cornwall: to Thomas Obourne, cutler of Salisbury: 31 May 1723. £24.

Colbourne Christopher, son of Thomas, mercer, deceased, late of Mere: to Edward Warren, stuffmaker of St. Philip and Jacob, Glos: 23 July 1712. £8.

Heart Elizabeth: to Daniel Dick, schoolmaster of Wroughton: 27 July 1759. £5.

Maundrell Robert son of Robert gent. of Compton Bassett: to James Baskerville, attorney of the Common Pleas, of Bristol. 27 August 1713 for 5 years. £100.

Potticary William to John Whitlock, woolstapler of Warminster. 6 May 1723. 4 years. £15.

PRO Ref. IR 1

hopefully trace them in another parish if they have been 'lost' or if the surviving parish registers and records do not happen to date back as far as 1664. The Hearth Tax exists for every county, but of course some may be in better condition than others.

The Apprentice Registers record payment of duties on apprenticeship indentures which came into force in 1710. They exist for all counties, but after 1760 the name of the apprentice's parent is not always given, nor is his address, and at times the master's trade is omitted as well. Apprenticeship records are an invaluable source for tracing an ancestor who may have been apprenticed to a master of mistress some distance from his or her home and on completion of apprenticeship may have decided to stay in that place, marry, and raise a family.

The PRO also issue a number of other leaflets on their collections, all free of charge. If sending by post a S.A.E. is required. Here follows an outline of each to give the reader an idea of their possible usefulness.

Leaflet No. 1 *Reprographic and Photographic Copies of Records in the Public Record Office.* Explains the rules regarding photographs and photocopies of records in the care of the PRO. It gives details of types of copying and current rates of charges.

Leaflet No. 2 *Charges for Photographs* (glossy type).

Leaflet No. 3 *Operational Records of the Royal Navy 1660-1914.* This is intended to provide guidance on records available relating to wartime operations and peaceful seafaring of the Royal Navy from 1660 to 1914.

Leaflet No. 4 *Sources for the History of the Jacobite Risings of 1715 and 1745.* This list contains both published and unpublished sources.

Leaflet No. 5 *Records of the Registrar General of Shipping and Seamen.* These records are a leading source of information for the history of British Merchant Shipping and sailors. There are two groups in this and one is on the ships and one on the sailors.

Leaflet No. 6 *Operational Records of the British Army in the 1914-18 War.* This leaflet is a guide to the records including the British Army, Dominion contingents, and Indian Army units under British command. These, however, do not include those concerned with administration, research and supply.

Leaflet No. 7 *Operational Records of the British Army during 1939-1945.* These only concern records relating to military operations of the British Army and its allies. Records concerning administration, supply, and research are mostly excluded. There are no personal records either, at the moment.

Leaflet No. 8 *H.M. Coastguard Records.*

Leaflet No. 9 *Division of Record Groups between Kew and Chancery Lane.* Lists the division of records between Chancery Lane and Kew, giving the letters of reference at the side of each class.

Leaflet No. 10 *Censuses of Population 1801-1881.*

Leaflet No. 11 *Records of the Royal Irish Constabulary.*

Leaflet No. 12 *Chancel Repairs.*

Leaflet No. 13 *Air Records as Sources for Biography and Family History.* The leaflet describes the main series of records concerning members of the Air Force, Royal Flying Corps and the Royal Naval Air Service.

Leaflet No. 14 *Family History in England and Wales (Guidance for Beginners).*

Leaflet No. 15 *Dockyard Employees (Documents in the PRO).*

Leaflet No. 16 *Operational Records of the Royal Air Force.* This is intended to give a brief outline of the main series of operational records of the RAF and its predecessors from the beginning of the First World War to the end of the Second. It does not include either personnel or technical records.

Leaflet No. 17 *Handbooks and Catalogues.* A short list of publications available for purchase from the PRO or government bookshops.

Leaflet No. 18 *Museum Publications.* A short list of catalogues, prints, posters, facsimiles of documents, and booklets available for purchase at the PRO and government bookshops.

Leaflet No. 19 *Postcards, Greetings cards and Notepads available from the PRO.*

Leaflet No. 20 *Replicas of Seals.* List of types and prices.

Leaflet No. 21 *List of 35mm Colour Transparencies Available from the PRO.*

Leaflet No. 22 *Records of the Foreign Office from 1782.* The records contained in this collection concern the period of time between its founding in 1782 and its amalgamation with the Commonwealth Office in 1968.

Leaflet No. 23 *Records of the American and West Indian Colonies before 1782.*

Leaflet No. 24 *English Local History.* A guide to help the researcher into local history records to prepare his or herself for a visit to the PRO.

Leaflet No. 25 *Copyright.* A list of guidelines only, not legal advice.

Leaflet No. 26 *Assize Records No. 1.*

Leaflet No. 27 *Hotels in the London Area, including Kew.*

Leaflet No. 28 *Genealogy before the Parish Registers.* A guide to the type of records available in the PRO prior to 1538.

Leaflet No. 29 *Royal Warrant Holders and Household Servants.* An introduction to the records of the Lord Chamberlain's and Lord Steward's Departments.

Leaflet No. 30 *Chancery Proceedings (Equity Suits).* From the fourteenth century until 1873, the court of Chancery handled disputes over inheritance, lands, marriage settlements, etc. This nine page booklet gives an insight into how and where to search for such records.

Leaflet No. 31 *Probate Records.* Where to look for a will or grant of administration. This, of course, refers to pre 1858 wills.

Leaflet No. 32 *British Transport Historical Records.* Records compiled by the British Transport Commission formerly housed in London, York, and Edinburgh. Covers records of Nationalized Railway Companies plus Canal, Dock and Shipping.

Leaflet No. 33 *The American Revolution.* Guides and lists to documents in the PRO.

Leaflet No. 34 *Land Grants in America and American Loyalists Claims.*

Leaflet No. 35 *How to use the Reading Rooms at Kew.*

Leaflet No. 36 *Means of Reference at Kew.*

Leaflet No. 37 *Access to Public Records.* A guide to when and which public records become available for public scrutiny.

Leaflet No. 38 *Change of Name.* How and where changes of name are recorded.

Leaflet No. 39 *Records of Births, Marriages and Deaths.* Not many records in these classes are kept by the PRO. This one is a pointer towards where you can find them.

Leaflet No. 40 *Enclosure Awards.* An explanation of how enclosures came about, and which records relating to the subject are likely to be found in the PRO.

Leaflet No. 41 *Tithe Records in the PRO.*

Leaflet No. 42 *Designs and Trademarks: Registers and Representation.* Records of the Patent Office and the Industrial Property Department of the Board of Trade which have now been transferred to the PRO including Registers and Representations of Designs and Trademarks. This leaflet should be studied well. It is a simple guide to what can be a rather complicated subject.

Leaflet No. 43 *Operational Records of the Royal Navy in the Second World War.*

Leaflet No. 44 *Apprenticeship Records as Sources for Genealogy in the PRO.*

Leaflet No. 45 *Markets and Fairs.*

Leaflet No. 46 *Militia Muster Rolls 1522-1640.*

Leaflet No. 47 *Are you in the Right Place? Census Returns,* Births, Marriages, Deaths and Wills, where they are to be found.

Leaflet No. 48 *Private Conveyances in the PRO.*

Leaflet No. 49 *Operation Records of the Royal Navy in the Great War, 1914-1919.*

Leaflet No. 50 *Records of the RAF in the PRO: Research and Development.*

Leaflet No. 51 *The Eccliastical Census of 1851.*

Leaflet No. 52 *Notes for New Readers at Chancery Lane.* A where and how guide for people who are new to the PRO system.

Leaflet No. 53 *Metropolitan Police Records of Service.*

Leaflet No. 54 *Registration of Companies and Businesses.*

Leaflet No. 55 *How to Read Roman Numerals.*

Leaflet No. 56 *Tax Records as a Source for Local and Family History c.1198 to 1698.*

Leaflet No. 57 *Information on the PRO.* An interesting leaflet describing not only the history and function of the organization, but it also gives dimensions and statistics.

Leaflet No. 58 *How to use the Census Room.*

Leaflet No. 59 *Sources of Bibliographical Information on Officers and Soldiers in the British Army.*

Leaflet No. 60 *Stationers' Hall Copyright Records.*

Leaflet No. 65 *Records Relating to Shipwrecks.*

Further reading

Tracing Your Ancestors in the Public Record Office by Jane Cox and Timothy Padfield (HMSO)
H.M.S.O. Guide to Public Record Office (3 Vols). (HMSO)
Records of Officers and Soldiers who have served in the British Army (HMSO)
Naval Records for Genealogists by N.A.M. Rodger (HMSO)
Irish History from 1700: Guide to Sources at the PRO by Alice Prochaska (British Records Assoc. Archives & the User Leaflet No. 6)
My Ancestor was a Merchant seaman — How can I find out more about him? by C.T. and M.J. Watts. (SOG 1936)
Chancery and Other Legal Proceedings by R.E.F. Garrett (Pinhorns 1968).
In addition to the books there is now a Public Record Office microfiche of their latest acquisitions which should be in most major reference libraries.

CHAPTER 14

Genealogical Societies, other Societies and Specialist Collections

Family history societies

Just about every county in England and Wales now boasts of at least one Family History Society. These are bodies formed by people interested in either one particular area for their research or who through enthusiasm for the subject join a family history society even though their roots may be in other areas. Many people belong to a number of societies. Membership usually costs only a few pounds annually and for this sum a person can expect to be offered a series of interesting talks by visiting speakers, a quarterly journal, and, perhaps, even the odd outing to places of interest. Out of county members are often helped with their research problems by members living in the locality, either free of charge or for a small payment to cover expenses, although much depends on local members having the time to help others. Most societies have projects in hand such as indexing census returns, parish registers and records, or monumental inscriptions. Such tasks have proved of tremendous help to fellow genealogists. Reciprocal research is another popular aid to family history research. In 1974 the Federation of Family History Societies came into being. This was a moulding together of the various county societies. The benefits gained from this have been many and varied. Twice each year a local family history society hosts a conference which is normally attended by between two and three hundred delegates and members. These are generally held over a weekend, and besides the annual general meeting of the Federation and its council, those attending are treated to a festival of lectures, static displays, and outings. To make sure it is a weekend to remember there is the Saturday evening banquet which usually enables everyone to forget their ancestors for a few hours. Another useful spin-off from the organization of the Federation is the large number of reasonably priced specialist books they publish.

Details of your local organization may be acquired by writing to the Administrator of the FFHS, The Birmingham and Midland Institute, Margaret Street, Birmingham, West Midlands B3 3BS. Please enclose a S.A.E. for a reply.

The Federation also publishes a twice yearly magazine, *Family History News and Digest,* this is particularly useful for those who wish to learn which subjects have been touched upon in the magazines published by local societies, as each issue contains an index to articles.

The Society of Genealogists

This society was founded as long ago as 1911. Its first meetings were held in a room on Fleet Street, London. This eventually became too small to hold its fast growing collection of genealogical books and papers, and after a few years in Bloomsbury they moved in 1931 to Chaucer House, Malet Street, London. the next move was in 1952 to larger premises in Harrington Gardens, and then finally to the present premises, a four-floored former silk warehouse in Charterhouse Buildings. The Society owns the largest collection of genealogical material and books in Britain. It has a 'giant card' index containing around 3,000,000 names, copies of parish registers, and a magnificent collection of *Boyd's Marriage Index* containing more that 6,000,000 marriage register entries. Also there is a marvellous collection of genealogical miscellany in Tract Boxes which are to be found on open shelves, and filed in alphabetical order. The complete run of the British IGI is available also. Many happy hours can be spent browsing in the library and one does not need to be a member, for a payment by the hour or day is possible. However, membership of the Society is highly recommended, especially if you intend to spend more than one day a year in the library. Those joining are entitled to receive copies of the Society's journal *The Genealogist's Magazine.* Another periodical is published for computer enthusiasts who are members of the society's computer group. A comfortable lounge is available for use by members and visitors where refreshments may be obtained at reasonable cost. There is a well-stocked book stall with a variety of genealogical books for sale, many of them being the Society's own publications. For full details of the Society and its holdings please send a S.A.E. to the Director, Society of Genealogists, 14 Charterhouse Buildings, Goswell Road, London, EC1M 7BA.

Other genealogical societies and journals

The Guild of One-Name Studies

This is a rapidly growing organization of one-name family history researchers or groups, i.e. The Palgrave FHS, The Copplestone FHS. A group is sometimes started off by just one person catching the imagination of others with the same name interests, and the society soon grows in numbers. To date, there are several hundred members of this one-name society — perhaps there is one already for your surname? A prospectus may be obtained by sending a S.A.E. to The Guild of One-Name Studies, Box G. 14 Charterhouse Buildings, Goswell Road, London, EC1M 7BA.

The Institute of Heraldic and Genealogical Studies

The organization of the Institute was largely due to the work of Mr Cecil Humphery-Smith. It was inspired by his godfather, Canon Julian Bickersteth, who unfortunately died in 1962, the year after its foundation. The Institute organizes family history courses, both residential and by post. It has a large collection of genealogical books and other material and publishes its own magazine *Family History*. Details of the organization may be obtained by sending a S.A.E. to The Institute of Heraldic and Genealogical Studies, 10 Northgate, Canterbury, Kent, CT1 1BA.

Family Tree Magazine

Family Tree first appeared in November 1984. Its circulation rapidly grew and now has readers in over 26 countries of the world. It is a lively publication catering for all family historians, beginner or expert alike. For details write to *Family Tree Magazine*, 141 Great Whyte, Ramsey, Huntingdon, Cambs. PE17 1HP.

Association of Genealogists and Record Agents

AGRA is the more popularly known term used for this organization. It was formed by and on behalf of professional genealogists in 1968. Membership of AGRA is limited to people who are able to prove, through example, that they are capable genealogists or record agents. The difference between the two is that a genealogist directs genealogical research on behalf of clients, whilst a record agent searches records specified by his client. Details and lists of members may be obtained from Mrs Jean Tooke, 1 Woodside Close, Caterham, Surrey, CR3 6AU.

Anglo-Jewish Association, Woburn House, Upper Woburn Place, London, WC1H 0EP.

This association is prepared to help with queries about Jewish ancestry, first make enquiries in writing. There is also a Jewish Museum at this address. See *Jewish Year Book* published by *The Jewish Chronicle Ltd.*

The Borthwick Institute of Historical Research, St Anthony's Hall, Peasholme Green, York YO1 2PW.

The archives are mainly those of the province and diocese of York, but also include parish records of the Archdeaconry of York, as well as other deposits. Enquiries in writing.

British Telecom Museum, Baynard House, 135 Queen Victoria Street, London, EC4V 4AT.

The museum houses the Historical Telephone Library with London and provincial telephone directories dating from 1880. First enquiries should be made to the Assistant Curator.

Congregational Library records are now administered by Dr Williams' Library, 14 Gordon Square, London, WC1H 0AG. (see Chapter 5).

English Catholic Ancestor

This society, formed in 1983, exists to promote interest in Catholic records and genealogy, but is open to anyone be they Catholic or not. Membership, which is very reasonably priced, is often worthwhile for those who are experiencing difficulty with Catholic ancestral connections. A list of current members is sent to all who join, and the services of honorary consultants are often available. A magazine is published twice a year. Details of membership may be obtained by sending a S.A.E. to the Honorary Secretary, Mr L. Brooks, Hill House West, Crookham Village, Aldershot, Hampshire, GU13 0SS.

The Guildhall Library, Aldermanbury, London, EC2P 2EJ.
The Guildhall Library is a reference library open to the public and which has numerous genealogical sources particularly for former inhabitants of the City of London. It holds a considerable quantity of material for the rest of England and some for the British Isles and overseas.

Irish Heritage Association, 164 Kingsway, Dunmurry, Belfast, BT17 9AD, N. Ireland.
Founded in 1981 by Mrs Kathleen Neill to provide as full a service as possible to those at home and abroad who wish to study their Irish Heritage. Their magazine *Irish Family Links* is available to members.

The Linen Hall Library, Wellington Place, Belfast 1, N.Ireland
Has early Irish newspapers, published Irish family histories and collection of family trees as well as local history societies magazines.

Methodist Archivist, John Rylands Library, Deansgate, Manchester, M13 9PL.
The archivist is prepared to supply the name and address of the honorary archivist of the required Methodist administrative area on receipt of a S.A.E. (see Chapter 5).

National Army Museum, Royal Hospital Road, London, SW3 4HT.
Although this is a museum, there is an extensive library for all those with military ancestry, including the Indian Army and Commonwealth Forces. Prior application for a reader's ticket to use the library facilities is needed.

National Library of Wales, Aberystwyth, Dyfed, SY23 3BU.
Reader's ticket is needed for entry to search rooms. Welsh genealogy records such as wills, administrations before 1858, Bishops Transcriptions for Wales, some parish and non-conformist registers, and the usual record office archives such as manorial, legal, estate and family records, are housed in this library.

National Maritime Museum, Romney Road, Greenwich, London, SE10 9NF.
This museum has a large library with a reference section, information service, and a fine collection of manuscripts. Apply first in writing for permission to use the library.

Public Record Office of Northern Ireland, 66 Balmoral Avenue, Belfast, BT9 6NY, N. Ireland.
The PRONI, as this office is more popularly called, contains records of Courts of Law, Government, and local authority departments, and other records deposited by institutions and individuals. It is advisable to visit out of the tourist season if possible. Public Record Office of Ireland (PROI). The Four Courts, Dublin, 7. Similar in content to the PRONI.

Royal Air Force Museum, Dept. of Aviation Records, Aerodrome Road, Hendon, London, NW9 5LL.

The library reading room here is open by appointment only.

Scottish Record Office, H.M. Register House, Princes Street, Edinburgh, EH1 3YY.

This is the repository for public records of Scotland, and includes almost all the surviving administrative archives of the ancient kingdom before the union of England and Scotland in 1707, as well as documents of the Courts of Law, legal records, and property.

The Irish Genealogical Research Society, 59/61 Pont Street, London, SW1.

The society has a small library at the Challoner Club and publishes a magazine entitled, *The Irish Genealogist.*

United Reformed Church History Society, 86 Tavistock Place, London, WC1H 9RT.

Arrangements must be made in writing before visiting this society. United Reformed Church archives include some Congregational material as well as Presbyterian records.

Bibliography

Specialist guides to useful information

A tremendous number of genealogical books have been published in Great Britain in the last few years, and people who are now just beginning to take an interest in the subject are far better off in this respect than those who started only ten years ago.

A Guide to Genealogical Sources in the Borthwick Institute of Historical Research by C.C. Webb (University of York 1982). ISBN 0305 8506. A useful guide to sources on how to trace a family tree in Yorkshire and some other northern counties.

A Study of the English Apothecary from 1660-1760 An informative and interesting publication by Juanita G. L. Burnaby, published in 1983 by the Wellcome Institute for the History of Medicine. ISBN 85484 0435.

Basic Sources for Family Historians. Back to the Early 1800s by Andrew Todd (Allen & Todd, Ramsbottom). A comprehensive booklet on the first steps of how to trace a family back to the 1800s.

Discovering your Family Tree by David Iredale and John Barrett (Shire Publications 4th ed. 1985). A pocket guide to tracing your ancestors and compiling your family history. ISBN 0 85263 7675.

English Parish Register Transcripts Edited by N. J. Vine-Hall (Society of Australian Genealogists 3rd ed. 1983). A list of all known transcripts of English parish registers held in Australian and New Zealand libraries. ISBN 0812 2881.

Family History — A Guide to Ayrshire Sources Published by the Ayrshire Archaeological and Natural History Society in 1984, and edited by Jane Jamison, this handbook is a useful aid to people starting out on their family research in the Ayrshire district of Scotland. Details available from the Reference Librarian, Main Street, Ayr, KA8 8ED.

Family History and Local History in England by David Hey. This book shows how to put genealogy into the context of the local historical setting of the family in question. Published by Longman. ISBN 058200 5200 5221.

Family History Annual 1986 This publication was originally intended to be the first of an annual series, but its editor, Michael Burchall, subsequently went to live in Thailand, so no further editions have appeared. The book is a compilation of medium length articles written by well known people in the family history world, on a wide range of subjects such as Scottish and Irish Records, the Poor Law Manorial Records. ISBN 0 907084.

Genealogical and Historical Map of Ireland (Heraldic Artists Ltd, Dublin). The distribution and location of Irish family names barony by barony and division of counties with an index. ISBN 09502455 6 9.

Genealogical Research Directory Published by Keith Johnson and Malcolm Sainty. This is an international compilation of annually subscribed ancestral names and researchers. Agents in various countries handle queries and sales. For Britain contact Mrs Elizabeth Simpson, Peapkins End, 2 Stella Grove, Tollerton, Nottingham, NG12 4EY. Most useful for putting people in touch with others researching the same name.

Genealogist's Bibliography by Cecil R Humphery-Smith. (Phillimore 1985). Bibliography of genealogical sources listed under counties, including a glossary of genealogical terms. ISBN 0 85033 422 5.

Genealogy in Ontario — Searching the Records by Brenda Dougall Merriman (Ontario Gen Society 1985). How to trace Ontario families in the Public Archives of Canada (PAC) and the Archives of Ontario (AO). ISBN 0 920036 16 3.

Guide to Genealogical Sources at the National Library of Wales (Dept of Manuscripts and Records, National Library of Wales, Aberystwyth 1986). How to make the best use of genealogical sources in the National Library of Wales.

Guide to the Parish Records of Clwyd This publication lists the available parish records of 148 parishes and chapelries throughout the modern Welsh county of Clwyd. It covers the old parishes of Denbighshire, Flintshire and part of Merioneth. Published by Clwyd County Council, and edited by A.G. Versey, the County Archivist. ISBN 0 905349 98 9.

Halfway to Writing a Family History by Ian Templeton (Pikers Pad, Storrington, Sussex 2nd ed. 1986). ISBN 0 90 7714 145. How to write and publish a family history.

Heraldry can be fun An economically priced handbook written by Iain Swinnerton and published by the Birmingham & Midland Society for Genealogy & Heraldry. Ideal for those who are trying to grasp the basics of the subject. ISBN 0 905 105 885.

In and Around Record Offices in Great Britain and Ireland by Rosemary Church and Jean Cole. A comprehensive guide to records offices, their facilities and local places of interest. (Wiltshire FHS 1987) ISBN 09512253 08.

Local Historian's Encyclopedia by John Richardson (Historical Publications Ltd, New Barnet, Herts, 2nd ed. 1986). ISBN 0 950 3656 7X. Although this book is entitled 'Local Historian's Encylopedia', it is a 'must' in every family historian's library as an invaluable reference.

Historical, Archaeological and Kindred Societies in the United Kingdom A list compiled by Malcolm Pinhorn (Pinhorns 1986). Includes lists of local and family history societies. ISBN 901 262 226.

History of Britain Edited by Kenneth O Morgan (Sphere publications). 3 Vols from c.55BC to 1983. Derived from the *Oxford Illustrated History of Britain,* these excellent books give an interesting and concise history of Britain for the family historian.

Libraries in the United Kingdom and the Republic of Ireland published by the Library Association and updated from time to time. This useful reference book can usually be found or obtained through your local library. It lists most main public libraries and many branches throughout Britain as well as more obscure specialist ones. ISBN 0 85365 916 8.

London's Local History Edited and published by Peter Marcan, this book deals with various categories of material overlooked or neglected by public libraries. It covers local history publications produced by non-commercial publishing organizations such as libraries and societies. ISBN 0 9504211 6 2.

Mac Roots by Tim Bede. Small in size, economical in price, this is a handbook of available sources north of the border. Published by MacDonald Edinburgh. ISBN 0 904265 684.

Manx Family Tree A beginners guide to records in the Isle of Man by Janet Narashimham, 1986. A comprehensive guide to sources in tracing family ancestry in the Isle of Man including a glossary of words and phrases relevant to the island.

National Genealogical Directory founded by Michael Burchall in 1979 and published annually, this lists subscribers to ancestral names. Another useful tool for putting people in touch with others with similar interests.

Old Title Deeds, A Guide for your Local and Family Historians by N W Alcock. This was first published by Phillimore in 1986. The author is of the opinion that although deeds are plentiful, they are nevertheless a rather neglected source of historical evidence. The aim of the book is to reveal how to extract the information contained in the documents without being overwhelmed by the legal jargon. ISBN 0 85033 595 0.

People Count — A History of the General Register Office by Muriel Nissel. An extremely informative book published by HMSO about the history of the General Register Office, civil registration and census returns. ISBN 0 11 6911832.

Reprographic Copying of Books and Journals British Copyright-Council. ISBN 0 901737. A guide for librarians, teachers, and all users of copyright works.

Searching Overseas — A Guide to Family History Sources for Australians and New Zealanders by Susan Pederson, published by Kangaroo Press. This book has been written for Australians and New Zealanders who are contemplating beginning the search for their roots in Australia, New Zealand and Great Britain. ISBN 0 86417 159 5.

Series of First Ordnance Survey Maps of England and Wales reproduced by David & Charles, Newton Abbot, Devon.

Simple Heraldry by Sir Iain Moncreiffe and Don Pottinger. First published in 1953, this book has seen many updates and revisions, the latest by John Bartholomew & Sons of Edinburgh. ISBN 0 7028 1009 6.

Special Indexes in Australasia A genealogists guide. If someone in your family tree went to live in that particular area, this little handbook could help to point you in the right direction. ISBN 0 958958 2 7. Details available from the compiler, Judy Webster, 77 Chalfont Street, Salisbury, Queensland 4107, Australia.

Ten London Repositories and *Six Kent Repositories* are two handy booklets published by Susan Bourne, the Kent genealogist. Both list various repositories in these areas and give a rundown of their contents, as well as useful information, like opening times, telephone numbers, how to get there and even toilet and coffee facilities. ISBN 0 9510678 3 4 and 0 9510678 1 8. Details from 26 Brookside Road, Istead Rise, Northfleet, Kent, DA13 9JJ.

The British Overseas A guide to records of their births, baptisms, marriages, deaths and burials available in the United Kingdom. Compiled by Geoffrey Yeo (Guildhall Library 1984). Guide to sources before c.1945 in the United Kingdom; some material in other countries is mentioned but not comprehensively.

Tracing Ancestors in North Staffordshire is another of those useful localized publications. It is edited by H. Eva Beech and published by the Birmingham & Midland Society for Genealogy & Heraldry. (3rd ed. 1988).

Tracing Your Bradford Ancestors was written and published in 1979 by Philip Rushworth, the Chairman of the Bradford Family History Society. Also by the same author are two more local publications, *Retracing your Bradford Ancestors* (1984) and *Tracing Your Calderdale Ancestors* (1980). Details available from the author at Arnside Cottage, Galloway Road, Greengates, Bradford, BD10 9AU, West Yorks.

Understanding the History and Records of Non-Conformity by Patrick Palgrave-Moore, published by Elvery Dowers 1987. A guide for beginners and more experienced researchers of family history to the complexities of non-conformists and their records. ISBN 09506290 4 9

Wakefield Court Rolls 1664-65 This ambitious project is being undertaken by the Yorkshire Archaeological Society. The series of publications are being issued in parts, each one listing thousands of names found in the Manor Court Rolls. Details may be obtained from the YAS, Claremont, Clarendon Road, Leeds LS2 9NZ.

Whereabouts of Yorkshire Parish Records Published by the Yorkshire Archaeological Society, Family History & Population Studies Section. A two-part series (part one A-J and part two K-Z) edited by Dr Ann Belt. Details available from YAS, Claremont, 23 Clarendon Road, Leeds, LS2 9NZ. ISSN 0265 119X.

Willings Press Guide This annual publication is to be found on most library shelves throughout Britain. It lists newspapers, both local and national, along with specialist and general magazines, their publishers, and, in many cases, their circulation figures. One very useful point mentioned is the date each publication first appeared.

Your Family History A general handbook for beginners, written by C.M. Mathews and published by Lutterworth Press. ISBN 0 7188 2542X.

Basic Sources for Family Historians (back to the early 1800s). Written by Andrew Todd, this is a practical, easy to follow publication, especially suitable for the complete beginner. Published by Allen and Todd. ISBN 0 948781 02 5.

Beginning Your Family History by George Pelling, former chairman of the FFHS. This is one of those publications which, although small in size and price, is large on information. An ideal handbook for the beginner. Published by Countryside Books and the FFHS. Hardback - ISBN 0 905392 91 4, available from bookshops. Paperback - ISBN 0 907099 63 7, available through family history circles.

British Archives A guide to archive resources in the United Kingdom by Janet Foster and Julia Sheppard. Published by Macmillan Reference Paperbacks. A survey of archive resources and an extensive and handy reference book directed at the general enquirer and researcher who needs to find out the extent of county record offices, repositories, libraries, and specialist and lesser-known institutions. The book contains details of collections and archives catering for the needs of the family historian in their various lines of research. The guide is arranged alphabetically by town and there are indexes to repositories, subjects and named collections. ISBN 0 333 378687.

Computers for Family History A most useful book to help the complete novice to understand the role computers can play in family history. Written in plain English by David Hawgood. Very helpful and informative. ISBN 0 948151 10 3.

Dictionary of Genealogy The contents of this very useful reference are gleaned from the notes taken over 25 years by professional genealogist T.V.H. Fitzhugh. It covers a wide range of words and subjects. Published by Alphabooks. ISBN 0 906670 38 1.

English Genealogy This 475 page volume, dealing with the social and economic background of English Genealogy, covers areas such as the Normans, the Huguenots and clergy, as well as migration and the aristocracy. The author, Sir Anthony Wagner, is one of Britain's foremost genealogists. Published by Phillimores. ISBN 0 85033 473 X.

Enjoying Archives by David Iredale, (214 pages). An introduction to archives in and around Great Britain. Pointing the way to many of the more unusual areas of research and at the same time giving helpful tips on how to make the best use of them. Published by Phillimore. ISBN 0 85033 561 2.

Tracing Your Family Tree

Family Historians Enquire Within A handy little booklet containing a vast amount of answers to those often-annoying words of which you don't know the meaning. Such as what are 'Pew Rents'? Or what is a 'Feoffee'? Published by the FFHS. ISBN 0 907099 41 6.

Family History in Focus Edited by Don Steel and Lawrence Taylor, this publication concentrates on the visual side of family history, going into much detail on the collection, identification, and preservation of photographs. A most practical and interesting book. Published by Lutterworth Press. ISBN 0 7188 2530 6.

Forming a One Name Group Written by Derek Palgrave and published by the FFHS, this booklet tells its readers all they need to know about how to start a one-name family history group. ISBN 0 907099 04 1.

Genealogy for Beginners There can be very few public libraries in Britain that do not have a copy of this evergreen on their shelves. Completely revised in 1984 by the author, A.J. Willis, assisted by Molly Tatchell. It was very sad that Mr Willis died before this revision appeared. Must be one of the all-time best sellers in genealogical circles. Published by Phillimore. ISBN 0 85033 346 6.

Greater Manchester Archives A guide to local repositories. The leaflets, are produced by the County District Archivist in Greater Manchester, and provide a brief guide to the location of archives in their area. Greater Manchester Record Office, 56 Marshall Street, New Cross, Manchester, M4 5FU.

Handbook on Irish Genealogy How to trace your ancestors and relatives in Ireland, 6th ed. Revised and edited by Donal F. Begley. One of the continuing guides on Irish research, this book's purpose is to give, as briefly as possible, all the facts about genealogical research in the Emerald Isle. It includes a series of 1837 Irish county maps and such items as emigrant passenger lists, nonconformist registers, American, Canadian, English, and Australian records and many other sources. Published by Heraldic Artists Ltd. ISBN 0 9502455 9 3.

How to Locate and use Manorial Records This booklet, written by Patrick Palgrave-Moore, describes manorial records and gives definitions of the manorial system and its officers and what information may be found in manorial documents. A long-awaited publication which shows how to compile and prove a family tree from manorial records. Published by Elvery-Dowers. ISBN 0 9506290 2 2.

How to Record your Family Tree Another of Patrick Palgrave-Moore's publications. This one explains the various ways of going about building a family tree. Especially helpful to the beginner. (Elvery-Dowers 1979).

How to Tackle Your Family History —A Preliminary Guide for the Beginner, (8 pages). Published by the FFHS. This pamphlet outlines an elementary guide to steps in tracing your family history with a 'Planning your Research' flow chart. ISBN 0 907099 24 6.

Huguenot Ancestry Written by Noel Currer-Briggs and Royston Gambier. This is a most interesting and informative publication, even if your ancestors were not Huguenots; even more so if they were. Published by Phillimores. ISBN 0 85033 564 7.

In Search of Scottish Ancestry A reasonably comprehensive guide to Scottish record sources. Covers both civil and parish records, as well as many of the more obscure archives north of the border. Written by Gerald Hamilton-Edwards, and published by Phillimores. ISBN 0 85033 513 2.

Irish Genealogy —A Record Finder Edited by Donal F. Begley. This is a sequel to the *Handbook of Irish Genealogy* (1980, 5th ed.) and consists of contributions from specialists on the subject, mainly from individuals connected with the Genealogical Office, and has chapters on Irish census returns and census substitutes; Irish directories and newspapers; wills and administrations etc. Published by Heraldic Artists Ltd. ISBN 0 950 2455 77.

Local History in England Although not written strictly for family historians, it is a very useful publication for filling in the background. It covers a great deal of the social history of our ancestors. Written by W. G. Hoskins and published by Longmans. ISBN 0 582 49371 4.

London Local Archives Published by the Guildhall Library and the Greater London Archives Network. This booklet is a guide for researchers to the archives and local history collections in the Greater London area. It does not list the holdings, but it does give readers details of the facilities in each office (i.e. the number of microform readers)and detailed instructions how to get there. Lists 39 offices. ISBN 0 900422 22 X (Guildhall), 0 9510665 0 1 (GLAN).

Location of British Army Records Norman Holding of the Bedfordshire Family History Society has earned himself a name as an expert on records of men serving in the British armed forces in World War One. This book is best read in conjunction with its sister publication, *World War 1 Army Ancestry.* Between them, one is able to gather a massive amount of information on available records and how to sort them out. Both published by FFHS.

More Sources of World War 1 Army Ancestry. Another of Norman Holding's valuable pointers to available records concerning soldiers who fought in the First World War. Published by the FFHS. ISBN 0 907099 61 0.

Naval Records for Genealogists by N.A.M. Rodger (Public Record Office publication HMSO 1984). A guide to official records of the Royal Navy of England, later Great Britain, concerned wholly or largely with officers and ratings.

Notes on Recording Monumental Inscriptions John Rayment's widely-acclaimed booklet on the subject covers a great many aspects of monumental inscriptions, including the famous 'peeping down tubes'. Published by FFHS. ISBN 0 907099 03 3.

Oral Evidence for the Family Historian Written by Lawrence Taylor, this publication gives advice on the collection and collation of material concerned mostly with the early part of one's family-history research. Published by FFHS. ISBN 0 907099 31 9.

Police History Monograph No.1. Notes for Family Historians by L.A. Waters (Police History Society 1987). An introductory guide for family historians who have family connections with the Police Service in England and Wales. ISBN 0 9512538 0 8.

Records of Officers and Soldiers who have served in the British Army A second edition (1985) of this inexpensive booklet explains the main series of records for the War Office and other government departments that are available in the Public Records Office. It provides information on officers and soldiers who have served in the British Army from 1660 to 1914 —from court martials to muster rolls; from Chelsea Pensioners to medals and awards; to returns of casualties and deserters. Published and printed by the Public Records Office, Ruskin Avenue, Kew, Richmond, Surrey TW9 4DU.

Register of One Name Studies 1987 The register contains names of societies, family associations and individuals who are interested in all references to a specific surname and its variants. Published by the Guild of One-Name Studies (4th ed.). ISBN 0 9508271 3 14.

Scottish Roots A step-by-step guide for ancestor-hunters in Scotland and overseas. This excellent book details the ancestor hunt from the beginning through to research at Scottish record offices and libraries. It includes case histories, overseas research without ever going to Scotland, and a chapter on folk museums for social background work. Written by Alwyn James. Published by MacDonald Edinburgh. ISBN 0 904265 46 3.

The Ancestor Trail in Ireland (A Companion Guide) This 32-page booklet although small in size is written by Donal F. Begley, and is comprehensively packed with notes for preparing to start on the 'ancestor trail'. It includes a map with counties, principal town and roads; a checklist of records to be searched; area registers of births, marriages, and deaths, and a list of county and town newspapers. Published by Heraldic Artists Ltd, Genealogy Bookshop, Trinity Street, Dublin 2, Ireland. ISBN 0 9502455 85.

The English Family 1450-1700 One of the series *Themes in British Social History* written by Ralph A. Houlbrooke. An enjoyable book in social history and a first-rate book for family historians who have traced their English forbears beyond the 1700s. It deals with all aspects of family life from 1450 to 1700. Published by Longman. ISBN 0 58249045 6.

The Family History Book Written by Stella Colwell, this is a good general text book. It covers many aspects of genealogy and a vast amount of subject matter. Published by Phaedon Press. ISBN 0 7148 2372 4.

The Family Tree Detective This manual is particularly helpful for solving genealogical matters, such as when one becomes 'stuck'. It covers the years from 1538 to the present. Published by Manchester University Press. ISBN 0 7190 0916 2.

The Parish Chest An extremely interesting and absorbing publication from which both local and family historians will find a tremendous amount of information and enjoyment. First published as long ago as 1946, this latest edition spreads to 369 pages of information on the parish and its records. Written by W.E. Tate, it is published by Phillimore. ISBN 0 85033 507 8.

The Phillimore Atlas and Index of Parish Registers Edited by Cecil Humphery-Smith. This must be one of the most comprehensive and detailed books around. It consists of a complete set of county maps containing parish boundary areas, a further set of old maps, and the second half of the book lists virtually every parish in English and Wales, giving the date of its records and where they and various transcripts can be found. No serious family historian should be without this publication. ISBN 0 11 440186 1.

Tracing your Ancestors in the Public Record Office A very comprehensive list of holdings in the PRO at Chancery Lane and Kew. Laid out in a way that is easy to follow. A most useful reference book. Compiled by Jane Cox and Timothy Padfield. Published by HMSO. ISBN 0 11 440186 1.

Tracing Your Family History Jean Cole, this book contains a wealth of information as to various sources available to your family-history research. One of those publications that will remain a useful text book for many years. Published by *Family Tree Magazine* ISBN 09511465 21.

Tracing your Family History in Australia A guide to sources. An informative 334-page guide on 'where-to-go-to-trace-ancestors' book. It is an up-to-date national summary of genealogical sources for each Australian state in 41 categories The book makes enjoyable reading and, for anyone seeking an ancestor who was a member of a razor-gang, a strumpet or bush ranger, this book tells you how to find such a person. The bibliography is comprehensive, as are the lists of published family histories and addresses of record locations. Written by Nick Vine-Hall. Published by Rigby. ISBN 0 7270 1953 8.

Writing a Family History A guide for family historians who wish to write and preserve the results of their research for future generations. It sets out in detail various ways and methods of how to write and publish a family history. Written by Dom Meadley. Published by Australian Institute of Genealogical Studies. ISBN 0 95931 48 6 5.

Gibson's Guides published by the Federation of Family History Societies

Of late, there has also been a noticeable trend in 'budget' type publications. Instead of being typeset by specialist typesetters, many such works are reproduced on machines varying from ordinary typewriters to home or commercial computers. One of Britain's leading exponents of this type of work is Jeremy Gibson, who, in the past few years, has produced many thousand such books — the well-known *Gibson's Guides*. Much of Jeremy's expertise in this field has also gone into helping with another useful set of publications, *The McLaughlin Guides*.

Both of these series of books represent excellent value for money. They are published by the Federation of Family History Societies at prices from around only £1. The Federation also publishes a number of other reasonably-priced titles by well-known people in the genealogical world, such as Norman Holding on Army records, and John Rayment on Monumental Inscriptions.

Bishops Transcripts and Marriage Licences This handy little booklet is compiled from information supplied by archivists and librarians. It gives a county-by-county guide to the whereabouts of the two classes of records in England, Wales and Ireland. ISBN 0 907099 12 2.

Census Returns 1841-1881 on Microfilm A genealogical guide through the counties of England and Wales, giving the whereabouts of the census return holdings. Only briefly mentions Scotland. ISBN 0 907099 19 X.

Coroner's Records in England and Wales The whereabouts of these records are of value to family historians in their research work. Written by Jeremy Gibson and Colin Rogers.

General Register Office and International Genealogical Indexes. Where to find them. This booklet incorporates the whereabouts of microfilm of birth, marriage and death indexes at St Catherine's House and the Mormon International Genealogical Index (IGI) ISBN 0 907099 73 4.

Hearth, Tax, other later Stuart Tax Lists and the Association Rolls The contents of this *Gibson Guide* are pretty well summed up in the title. Another excellent pointer in the right direction if you are interested in these particular sources. ISBN 0 907099 34 2.

Land and Tax Assessments 1690-1950 Edited by Jeremy Gibson and Dennis Mills, this booklet tells how to find and make the best use of land-tax assessments on a county-by-county basis. ISBN 0 907099 22 X.

Local Newspapers 1750-1920; England & Wales, Channel Islands and Isle of Man; A Select Location List Compiled by Jeremy Gibson (FFHS 1987). Comprehensive guide to location of newspapers which survived more than four years. ISBN 0 907099 46 7.

Marriage Census and other Indexes for Family Historians An amalgamation of two earlier very popular *Gibson Guides.* Another county-by-county guide giving details of where the indexes to both popular records such as marriages, and some lesser-known ones like parish-assisted emigrants or Quakers can be found. ISBN 0 907099 29 7.

Probate Jurisdictions A simplified guide to the often complicated subject of probate records. A good glossary introduces the book, which gives the reader comprehensive advice on where to find the records throughout Great Britain. ISBN 0 907099 45 9.

Quarter Sessions Records for Family Historians An excellent publication designed to point researchers to a very often overlooked but sometimes valuable source of information. Covers the counties of England and Wales. Names a wide variety of types of records to be found, such as licensing, jurors and poll books to name only three. ISBN 0 907099 26 2.

Record Offices and How to Find Them This guide was compiled with the help of Pamela Paskett and has recently been revised. The addresses of the record offices throughout England and Wales are accompanied by clearly-drawn maps of the area around each one. The book also contains a list of some 'Do's' and 'Don'ts' and a map of the ancient counties of England and Wales. ISBN 0 907099 40 8.

Unpublished Personal Name Indexes in Record Offices And Libraries This first appeared in 1985,and has been reprinted and updated again. The purpose of the guide is to help researchers to find classes of records not already covered by the earlier *Gibson Guides*. Mentioned are things like Apprentices, Marriage Indexes, Lay Subsidy, and Manor Court Rolls, as usual in a county-by-county order. ISBN 0 907099 35 1.

The McLaughlin Guides Published by the Federation of Family History Societies

Annals of the Poor An extremely useful guide to a very interesting and absorbing aspect of family history. Most family historians sooner or later come across a pauper in their researches. Among the subjects Eve McLaughlin explains are the parish poor and how the money was raised to help them. About the settlement rules, bastardy, crime, workhouses, and the New Poor Law. ISBN 0 907099 55 6.

Family History from Newspapers A more than useful little guide for family historians on how to use newspapers to discover more. It covers the history and what exactly newspapers have in store for the researcher. ISBN 0 907099 70X

Illegitimacy This little book tells the reader, among other things, why some bastards are better off than others. It goes into the social background of the subject, and also explains the system of bastardy bonds, as well as how to extract information from sources such as parish registers and official records. ISBN 0 907099 38 6.

Interviewing Elderly Relatives One of the very first things a beginner should do is talk to as many elderly relatives as possible. Some like being asked family questions; some resent it very much. This booklet gives a wide range of ideas on how to approach the subject. There are many tips on the sort of questions to ask, and how to ask them. ISBN 0 907099 39 4.

Parish Registers Another basic guide to a useful source. This one covers many aspects connected with the subject, such as the dates, the Hardwicke Act, Non-conformists and Catholics, Quakers, Jews, and Bishop's Transcripts, to name only a few. Scotland and Irish registers also get a mention. ISBN 0 907099 56 4.

Reading old Handwriting (FFHS 1987). Illustrated guide on how to read old handwriting from the Victorian and Elizabethan eras. ISBN 0 907099 62 9.

St Catherine's House This one explains the civil registration as set up in 1837. It gives a comprehensive explanation of the system used, and gives the beginner a good basic grounding for a first visit to St Catherine's House. Scotland, Ireland and adoptions are also touched upon, as are miscellaneous registers. ISBN 0 907099 36 X.

Simple Latin We all come across Latin in the older parish registers, and most of us can pick out a few words and make sense of them. This helpful little guide will enlighten its reader even more. ISBN 0 907099 58 0.

Somerset House Wills from 1858 As the title implies, this booklet tells us about the contents of Somerset House. It also goes into the system used there. Added for good measure, are sections describing wills and 'admons', lapsed legacies, married women's property, intestacy, and district probate registries and indexes. ISBN 0 907099 37 8.

The Censuses 1841-1881 — Use and Interpretation The title says most of what the book contains. It does, however, go a little deeper into the subject, and also gives the beginner a few tips on how to approach the system in the Census Office in Portugal Street. ISBN 907099 49 1.

Wills before 1858 The tracing of pre-1858 wills is sometimes a pretty complicated subject. This little book will help its readers to get a clearer picture, as well as explaining the way old wills are composed. ISBN 0 907099 50 5.

Society of Genealogists' publications
The Society of Genealogists is another publisher of reasonably-priced and useful publications. Although some of theirs are guides to material in the Society's library, a number of others are very helpful with specific lines of inquiry, such as *My Ancestors were Quakers, how can I find more out about them?*

Examples of Handwriting 1550-1650 Compiled by W.S.B. Buck (SOG 1985). A wide variety of letters of the alphabet, abbreviations, and 'confusabilia' have been compiled in this handy reference book. ISBN 0 901878 54 5.

Greater London Cemeteries and Crematoria Compiled by Patricia S. Wolfston (SOG 1985). How to locate nineteenth century burial places in the Greater London area. ISBN 0 901878 67 7.

My Ancestor was a Baptist By Geoffrey R. Breed (SOG 1986). Biographical information regarding Baptist ancestors including a complete list of registers and records in the P.R.O., Chancery Lane, London. ISBN 0901878 84 7.

My Ancestor was Jewish — How can I find out more about him? Edited by Michael Gandy (SOG 1982). Sources to Jewish ancestry research — bibliographies, census returns, denixation papers, surnames etc.

My Ancestor was a Merchant Seaman — How can I find out more about him? By Christopher T. and Michael J. Watts. (SOG 1986). ISBN 0 901878 73 1. (A range of possible sources for merchant navy ancestry).

My Ancestor was a Methodist — How can I find out more about him? By Rev. William Leavy, edited by Michael Gandy (SOG 1982). A guide to Methodist source material, registers, biographies, minute books etc. ISBN 0 901878 49 9.

My Ancestor was a Migrant (in England and Wales). How can I find where he came from? by Anthony J. Camp. An extensive listing of sources available to find a missing ancestor from solicitors to poor wives of soldiers to tobacco pipe-makers to army and navy men. ISBN 0 901878 944.

My Ancestor was a Quaker — How do I find out more about him? An outline of 'Friends' meetings in Great Britain and Ireland for church affairs together with main classes of records to about 1850. ISBN 0 901878 59 6.

Monuments and their Inscriptions A practical guide by H. Leslie White (SOG 1978). How to record, equipment needed, the law, co-operations and co-ordination on recording monumental inscriptions. ISBN 0 901878 35 9.

National Index of Parish Registers — (whereabouts of original registers, transcripts and Bishops Transcripts).

> Vol 1 — Sources for Births, Marriages and Deaths before 1837. (1976) Parish registers, ancillary and medieval sources bibliography.
>
> Vol 2 — Sources for Non-conformist Genealogy and Family History (1973).
>
> Vol 3 — Sources for Roman Catholic and Jewish Genealogy and Family History.
>
> Vol 12 — Sources for Scottish Genealogy and Family History.
>
> Vol 4 — Kent, Surrey, Sussex (1980).
>
> Vol 5 — Gloucestershire, Herefordshire, Oxfordshire, Shropshire, Warwickshire, Worcestershire (1976).
>
> Vol 6 — Part 1 Staffordshire (1982).
>
> Vol 7 — East Anglia, Cambridgeshire, Norfolk, Suffolk (1983).
>
> Vol 11 — Part 1 Durham, Northumberland (2nd ed. 1984).
>
> Vol 13 — Parish Registers of Wales (1986).

Everyone Has Roots Written by the Director of the Society of Genealogists, A.J. Camp (1978). The Society has also published a series of twenty-three leaflets giving advice to beginners.

Other useful publications

More books in brief, many are now out of print, but perhaps available through your public library service.

Introduction to Archives G. Emmison. Phillimore. 1974.

A Shepherd's Life W.H. Hudson. Macdonald. 1981.

Agricultural Revolution Chambers and Mingay. 1968.

Alumni Cantabrigiensis (10 Vols). J.A. Venn.

Alumni Oxoniesis 1500 to 1886 (8 Vols). J. Foster.

Archives and Local History F.G. Emmison. Phillimore. 1974.

Bid Time Return (A Family History place, with script, story, documents and video) Beryl Hurley and Jean Cole (Wiltshire FHS 1987).

Canal Boatmen 1760 to 1914 Harry Hanson. 1984.

Canals of the British Isles (Series) Charles Hadfield. David and Charles.

Coaching Life: Heyday of Coach Travel in Britain Harry Hansen. 1983.

Complete Guide to Heraldry A.C. Fox-Davies. Nelson. 1969.

Costumes of Everyday Life 900 to 1910 Margot Lister. Barrie and Jenkins. 1972.

Crime in Early Modern England 1550 to 1750 J.A. Sharpe. 1984.

Dictionary of Heraldry C.N. Elvin. *Heraldry Today.* 1986.

Discovering Heraldry J. Fearn. Shire Publications. 1980.

Discovering Your Family History Don Steel. BBC Publications. 1986.

Domesday Book: England's Heritage, Then and Now Thomas Hinde. Hutchinson. 1985.

Domesday Books for Counties in England (Series) Phillimore.

Drovers Shirley Toulson. 1985.

Early Factory Acts and Their Enforcement Ursula R.Q. Henriques. Historical Association. 1971.

Education of People Mary Sturt. RKP. 1967.

Eighteenth Century England Dorothy Marshall. Longman. 1982.

Elementary Education in the 19th Century Gillian Sutherland. Historical Association. 1982.

Encyclopedia of Dates and Events Hodder and Stoughton. 1981.

England's Apprenticeship 1603-1763 Charles Wilson. Longman. 1984.

English Alehouse: A Social History 1200 to 1830 Peter Clark. 1983.

English Countryman and English Countrywoman (2 Vols). G.E. Fussell. Bloomsbury Books. 1985.

English Land Tax in the 18th Century W.R. Ward. Oxford University Press. 1953.

English Local Government in the 19th and 20th Centuries B. Keith Lucas. Historical Association. 1977.

English Parish Church and the Local Community G.H. Bettey. Historical Association. 1985.

English Yeoman in the Tudor and Stuart Age Mildred Cambell. 1974.

Family House in England Andrew Henderson. Phoenix House. 1964.

Farm and Cottage Inventories F.W. Steer. 1974.

Genealogical Atlas of England and Wales Smith and Gardner. 1960.

Genealogical Research in England and Wales (3 Vols). Smith and Gardner. Bookcraft USA.

Handbook of Dates C.R. Cheney. Royal Historical Society. 1978.

HMSO Guide to Official Sources: Census Reports of GB. HMSO. 1951.

How to Read a Coat of Arms Peter Summers.1986.

How to Read Local Archives 1550 to 1700 F.G. Emmison. Phillimore. 1967.

How to Trace Family History in N. Ireland Kathleen Neill. Irish Heritage Assoc. 1986.

How to Trace Your Ancestors Meda Mander. Mayflower. 1977.

Huguenot Heritage Robin Gwynn. RKP. 1985.

Illustrated Journeys of Celia Fiennes Circa 1682 - 1712 Christopher Morris. Macdonald. 1984.

In Search of Army Ancestry G. Hamilton-Edwards. Phillimore. 1977.

In Search of Welsh Ancestry G. Hamilton-Edwards. Phillimore. 1986.

Indexes to Changes of Name 1760 - 1901 Phillimore and Fry. Phillimore. 1986.

Irish and Irish Scots Ancestral Research M. Dixon Falley. 1961.

Irish Families and More Irish Families B. Maclysaght. Irish University Press. 1983.

Latin for Local History Eileen Gooder. Longman. 1979.

Lay Subsidies and Poll Taxes M.W. Beresford. Phillimore. 1963.

Local Community and the Great Rebellion A.M. Everitt. Historical Association. 1969.

Making a Pedigree John Unett. 1987.

Manorial Records P.D.A. Harvey. British Records Association No. 5. 1984.

Men Who Built Railways Condor and Simmons. 1983.

Old Village Life P.H. Ditchfield. E.P. Publishing Ltd. 1974.

Our Forgotten Past: Seven Centuries of Life on the Land Jerome Blum. 1982.

Oxford Dictionary of English Christian Names E.G. Withycombe. Clarendon Press. 1977.

Packmen, Carriers and Packhorse Roads D. Hey. 1980.

Place Names Series Volume for each county. Cambridge University Press.

Poor Law in Nineteenth Century England A. Digby. 1982.

Poverty and Vagrancy in Tudor England John Pound. Longman. 1986.

Problem of the Poor in Tudor and Early Stuart England A.L. Bier 1983.

Railway Workers 1849 to 1870 F. McKenna.

Records of Naval Men G. Fothergill. 1910.

Recusant History — Post Reformation Catholic History Anthony J. William. Catholic Records Vol. 16 No 4. 1983.

Rural Life in Victorian England G.E. Mingay. Heinemann. 1977.

Rural World 1780 to 1850 Pamela Horn. Hutchinson. 1980.

Scottish Family Histories Joan Ferguson. Edinburgh. 1986.

Secretary Hand ABC Book Alf Ison. Tilehurst Reading Berks.

Shopkeeper's World 1830 to 1914 M.J. Winstanley. 1983.

Simple Guide to Irish Genealogy Rosemary Folliot. Irish Genealogical Research.

Skilled Labourer J.L. and B. Hammond. Longman.

Social History of England Asa Briggs. Penguin. 1985.

Something to Declare — 1000 Years of Customs and Excise G. Smith. 1980.

Tithes and the Tithe Commutation Act of 1836 E.J. Evans. Bedford Sq. Press. 1978.

Title Deeds A.A. Dibben. Historical Association. 1968.

Town Labourer J.L. and B. Hammond. Longman.

Town Records John West. 1984.

Tracing Your Ancestors Marilyn Yurdan. David and Charles 1988.

Trade Union and Related Records Bennet and Story. 1981.

Urban Poverty in Britain 1830 to 1914 J.H. Treble. 1983.

Village Labourer J.L. and B. Hammond. Longman.

Village Life in England 1860 to 1940 Brown and Ward. 1985.

Village Records John West. Macmillan. 1962.

Welsh Surnames (A Book of) T.R. Davies. Sheppard Press. 1952.

Workhouse System 1834 to 1929 M.A. Crowther. 1983.

World We Have Lost Peter Laslett. 1971.

Worldwide Family History N. Currer-Briggs. RKP. 1982.

Writing Local History: A Practical Guide D. Dymond. BALH Bedford Sq. Press. 1982.

Your Irish Ancestors J.A. Black. Paddington Press. 1974.

Glossary

Abstract. Abbreviation of a document containing the essential details.
Affadavit. Written declaration on oath.
Ag. Lab. Agricultural Labourer.
Allegation. Statement made on oath.
Anabaptist. When found in parish registers usually refers to a Baptist or a Quaker — Derogatory term.
Archive. Ancient and Historical Record.
Badgeman. A person responsible for ensuring all paupers receiving parish relief wore badges.
Badger. Pauper — from the badge a pauper was obliged to wear on his clothing.
Badger. Licensed Beggar: Pedlar: Chapman.
Bargain and Sale. Conveyance of estate for money.
Brewster Sessions. Annual sessions held to license victuallers from 1729.
Bridewell. Early gaol or house of correction.
Brief. Letter commending a charitable appeal (ecclesiastical or civil).
Calendar. A precis full enough for most purposes to replace original documents.
Canon Law. Church law.
Catalogue. Calendar or descriptive list containing records of similar content drawn from different groups or classes.
Chattels. Personal goods.
Churching of Women. Ceremony of purification after the birth of a child.
Codicil. An addition to a will — signed and witnessed.
Consanguinity. Of the same blood — related by birth.
Cordwainer. Shoemaker, originally one who used cordova leather.
Curtilage. Small courtyard or piece of ground attached to a dwelling house.
Dame School. Elementary school run by women for a small fee.
Deposition. Testimony given under oath in a court (church or law).
Descriptive List. List with brief abstract of documents.
Diocese. Area of a Bishop's jurisdiction.
Dissenters. Those who did not conform to the established Church of England.
Emigrant. Person leaving a country to live elsewhere.

Executor: Executrix. Man or woman appointed by testator to ensure the provisions of a will are carried out.

Facsimile. An exact copy.

Farlieu. Money payment.

Foundling. Abandoned infant usually in a public place.

FWK. Framework knitter — a worker in the hosiery trade.

Genealogy. Pedigree of a person or family — study of descent of a family from an ancestor.

Glebe Terrier. Survey of church lands and benefices.

Gossips. Godparents.

Half-baptized. Baptized privately.

Hundred. Administrative division of a county.

Husbandman. Small farmer, usually tenant farmer.

Immigrant. Person coming into a country to settle.

Incumbent. Parson; Vicar; Rector; Perpetual Curate.

Indenture. Deed entered into between two or more parties, each party having a copy.

Index. Alphabetically arranged references to people, places or subjects mentioned in records.

Interregnum. The time between two reigns; the time between the cessation of one and the establishment of another government.

Intestate. Died without leaving a will.

Journeyman. One whose apprenticeship was complete and who hired his labour out by the day.

Nephew. Until end of the seventeenth century meant a grandson or kinsman.

Niece. Until seventeenth century very often used to denote younger female relative.

Paleography. The study of old handwriting.

Petty Sessions. Meeting of two or three local magistrates for local business.

Poll Tax. Tax levied on the population.

Presentment. Statement of fact made on oath (Churchwardens in Bishop's or Archdeacon's correctional courts) also other courts.

Ragged School. School for poor children — free for the poorer children.

Recognizance. Legal document with certain stated conditions to ensure appearances at quarter sessions.

Recusants. Non-conformists, especially Roman Catholics; those who did not attend the Anglican Church.

Relict. Widow.

Sojourner. Temporary resident in a parish.

Special Sessions. Held monthly in each division of a county informal meetings by magistrates.

Spurious. Illegitimate child.

Stray. Record of a person found in a place other than his place of birth or settlement.

Substitute. Person provided by a person or parish to replace parishioner balloted for service in the militia.

ALPHABETS from A. Wright's *Court Hand Restored* (5th ed., 1816, plates 18, 19), illustrating a variety of forms of letters, mainly but not entirely from 16th and 17th century Legal and Chancery hands.

A general alphabet of the Old Law Hands

Surrogate. Deputy, also deputy of a Bishop.

Terrier. Register or roll of a landed estate; inventory.

Testamentary. Pertaining to a testament or will.

Testator. One who leaves a will.

Transcript. Exact text of an original manuscript or document.

Tyburn Ticket. Exemption certificate from a parish office; for capture, successful prosecution and conviction of a felon.

Vagrant. Person with no fixed abode.

Yeoman. Freeholder or occupying owner who farms his own land.

Appendix

Some useful dates for the family historian

1534	Act of Supremacy — Henry VIII becomes Head of the English Church.
1536	Union of Wales with England.
1538	Commencement of parish registers — all christenings, marriages, and burials to be recorded in a book to be kept in a 'sure coffer'.
1563	Roman Catholic Church ordered registers of baptisms and marriages to be kept.
1597/8	Parish registers to be kept in parchment book. Copies of each year's entries to be sent to the diocesan registry within a month after Easter. These copies are known as Bishops' Transcripts or BTs.
1601 & 1640	Poor Law Acts.
1653	Interregnum government took over the custody of parish registers and appointed clerks to keep them. All wills to be proved in the Prerogative Court of Canterbury — this was abolished upon the restoration of the monarchy in 1660.
1662-1689	Hearth Tax. Those on poor relief or in houses worth less than 20/- over year and not paying parish rates were exempt. Rate paid was 2/- a hearth.(Surviving records 1662-1674).
1662 & 1697	Settlement Acts. No stranger to enter a parish unless they possessed a settlement certificate and were able to maintain themselves. If unable to maintain themselves they were to be removed back to parish of settlement which was not necessarily their parish of origin.
1667 & 1678	Burial in Wool Acts. Legislation in 1667 but was more strictly enforced in 1678. Acts were repealed in 1814 although burial in wool had fallen into disuse long before this date.
1692	Land Tax. Became perpetual in 1797 and lasted until 1831. Rate usually around 4/- in the pound.

1694	Parliament taxed births, marriages and burials as registered in parish registers, also widowers without children and bachelors, to raise War revenue. 1695 — with penalty clauses. Repealed after a few years.
1696	Window Tax.
1707	Union of England and Scotland.
1710	Stamp duty on apprentice indentures — did not apply to parish or pauper apprentices.
1722/3	Parishes encouraged to build workhouses.
1751/2	Lord Chesterfield's Act. Change of calendar from Julian to Gregorian calendar. Year to commence 1st January through to 31st December.
1753/4	Hardwicke's Marriage Act — to end clandestine marriages. All marriages to be performed in Church of England by ministers of the church by banns or licence. Jews and Quakers excluded from the Act — all other non-conformist sects including Roman Catholics had to conform. Implemented in 1754.
1760-1797	Enclosure Acts-about 1500 private enclosure acts passed.
1777-1852	Male Servants Tax-employers only named.
1778	Catholic Relief Act — Roman Catholics allowed to own land again after taking oath of allegiance.
1783	Tax on all baptisms, marriages and burials. Paupers exempt. Repealed in 1794.
1785-1792	Female Servants Tax — employers only named.
1795	Speenhamland system of outdoor relief adopted-wages made up to equal cost of subsistence.
1801	Union with Ireland. First British Census.
1801	General Enclosure Act.
1812	Parochial Registers Act — Rose's Act. Enforced 1813. Three separate registers for baptisms, marriages and burials. Entries for baptisms to include names, address, description of parents. burial entries to include age, abode and name of deceased.
1823	Marriage Act — any clandestine marriages were now valid — that is, all those which had taken place without banns or licence, but the officiating minister was to be declared a felon.
1829	Catholic Emancipation — most restrictions now lifted.
1832	Parliamentary Reform Act.
1834	Poor Law Amendment Act — encouraged parishes to combine into Unions to provide workhouses for the poor.
1836	Enclosure by consent — enclosure without private legislation if two-thirds of the interested parties agreed.
1836	Tithe Commutation Act. Converted payment of tithes into an annual rent. Tithe maps date around 1838-1854.
1837	Civil Registration — 1 July 1837. Registration in England and Wales — all births, marriages and deaths to come under control of the State and to be registered with the Civil Registrars

appointed and all returns of births, marriages and deaths to be sent to the Registrar General.

1837	Commission appointed to call in all existing non-parochial registers.
1840	Non-parochial Register Act — surrendered registers of non-conformists deposited in the General Registrar's Office.
1841-1881	Census Returns — taken every ten years from 1801 except for 1941. Available to the public after 100 years. First census of use to family historian is that of 1841.
1845	Enclosure Acts — authorized Enclosure Commissioners to consider applications for enclosure — also gave Commissioners power to allocate land for 'exercise and recreation'.
1851	Ecclesiastical Census — listed every place of worship with signature of incumbent or clerk at end of each return. (Valuable for non-conformist chapels which have either disappeared or have been amalgamated).
1852/3	Burial Acts. Local authorities to administer cemeteries as churchyards were overcrowded.
1855	General Registration of births, marriages and deaths commenced in Scotland.
1857	Probate Act. All wills and administrations to be proved at the Principal Probate Registry, Somerset House, London, for England and Wales commencing 1858.
1864	General Registration of births, marriages and deaths commenced in Ireland.
1876	Curtailment of enclosures.
1882/3	Married Women's Property Act — married women finally to have control over their own property and money and now allowed to make wills.
1926	Adoption of children legalized in England.
1929	Marriage Act. Age of marriage with consent of parents or guardians raised to age of 16 years for boys and girls. Previously boys were able to marry at 14 years of age and girls at 12 years of age with consent of parents or guardians.

Some miscellaneous terms

c.	Circa (about) — used in conjunction with dates Example c.1645 — about 1645.
C or Cent.	Century
Co-h.	Co-heir/co-heiress
Ct.	Court
Dat.	Dated
H	Heir/Heiress
IA	Amongst others

Lady Day	25 March (until 1752 was the start of the new year)
Michaelmas	29 September
N	Natal or birth date
QV	Which see
S & H	Son and heir
Sic	As written but appears to be incorrect
Temp	Time of — Example Temp Henry VIII

Abbreviations and colloquialisms used in family history

'Blanket search'	A search, usually in parish registers or bishops transcripts taking every entry for a family surname
BMD	Births, marriages and deaths
Boyds	Marriage Index compiled by Percival Boyd for selected parishes
BTs	Bishops' Transcripts
Chancery Lane	The Public Record Office, Chancery Lane, London
CMB	Christenings (baptisms), marriages and burials
Colindale	British Museum Newspaper Library, Colindale, London
CRO	County Record Office, sometimes referred to by its location i.e. Trowbridge — Wilts Record Office or WRO.
Dissenter	See Non-conformist
DRO	Diocesan Record Office
Federation (FFHS)	Federation of Family History Societies
FHS	Family History Society
GRD	Genealogical Research Directory
Hardwicke's	Hardwicke's Marriage Act 1753 — an act for the prevention of clandestine marriages
IGI	The International Genealogical Index, formerly the Computer File Index. Microfiche records of births, baptisms and marriages compiled by the Church of Jesus Christ of Latter Day Saints or Mormons
Kelly's	Publisher of one of a series of directories. Other publishers — Billing, Pigot, White, Post Office etc.
Kew	The Public Record Office, Kew, Surrey
LDS	Church of Jesus Christ of Latter Day Saints
MIs	Monumental Inscriptions (on gravestones and memorials in churches)
NGD	National Genealogical Directories — series of directories containing family historians' surname interests
NLW	National Library of Wales
NS	New Style (Gregorian calendar)

Non-conformists or Dissenters	Those whose faith does not conform to the established Church of England
Non-parochial records	Records of denominations other than those of the Church of England — non-conformist records
OS	Old Style (Julian calendar)
Parish Chest	A chest used as a repository for parish records of a church — term still used for parish records
PCC	Prerogative Court of Canterbury
PCY	Prerogative Court of York
Phillimore	Publisher of marriage entries from selected parish registers
Portugal Street	The Public Record Office, Land Registry Building, Portugal Street, London (Census)
PPR	Principal Probate Register Office, Somerset House, London, (Wills from 1858)
PRs	Parish registers
PRO	Public Record Office
Rose's	Rose's Act of 1812 — new form of parish register books for baptisms and burials from 1813
St Catherine's	General Register Office of GRO for Births, marriages and deaths from 1837 — also miscellaneous registers
SOG	Society of Genealogists
Somerset House	The Principal Probate Registry — Wills from 1858 Records of divorce (Divorce Registry)
Three Dominations	Main non-conformist churches — Presbyterian, Baptist and Congregational
VCH	Victoria County History — series of histories of English counties

Registration district reference numbers at the General Register Office, St. Catherine's House, 10 Kingsway, London

1837 to 1851		**1852 to 1946**	
Anglesey	XXVII	Anglesey	11b
Bedfordshire	VI	Bedfordshire	3b
Berkshire	VI	Berkshire	2c
Brecknockshire	XXVI	Brecknockshire	11b
Buckinghamshire	VI	Buckinghamshire	3a
Caernarvonshire	XXVII	Caernarvonshire	11b
Cambridgeshire	XIV	Cambridgeshire	3b
Cardiganshire	XXVII	Cardiganshire	11b
Carmarthenshire	XXVI	Carmarthenshire	11a

Cheshire	XIX	Cheshire	8a
Cornwall	IX	Cornwall	5c
Cumberland	XXV	Cumberland	10b
Denbighshire	XXVII	Denbighshire	11b
Derbyshire	XIX	Derbyshire	7b
Devonshire	IX,X	Devonshire	5b
Dorsetshire	VIII	Dorsetshire	5a
Durham	XXIV	Durham	10a
Essex	XII	Essex	4a
Flintshire	XIX,XXVII	Flintshire	11b
Glamorgan	XXVI	Glamorgan	11a
Gloucestershire	XI,XVIII	Gloucestershire	6a
Hampshire	VII,VIII	Hampshire	2b,2c
Herefordshire	XXVI	Herefordshire	6a
Hertfordshire	VI	Hertfordshire	3a
Huntingdonshire	XIV	Huntingdonshire	3b
Kent	V	Kent	2a,1d
Lancashire	XX,XXI,XXV	Lancashire	8b,8c,8d,8e
Leicestershire	XV	Leicestershire	7a
Lincolnshire	XIV	Lincolnshire	7a
London (with suburbs)	I,II,III,IV	London(with suburbs)	1a,1b,1c,1d
Merionethshire	XXVII	Merionethshire	11b
Middlesex	I,II,III	Middlesex	1a,1b,1c,1d,3a
Monmouthshire	XXVI	Monmouthshire	11a
Montgomeryshire	XXVII	Montgomeryshire	11b
Norfolk	XIII	Norfolk	4b
Northamptonshire	XV	Northamptonshire	3b
Northumberland	XXV	Northumberland	10b
Nottinghamshire	XV	Nottinghamshire	7b
Oxfordshire	XVI	Oxfordshire	3a
Pembrokeshire	XXVI	Pembrokeshire	11a
Radnorshire	XXVI	Radnorshire	11b
Rutland	XV	Rutland	7a
Shropshire	XXVI,XVIII	Shropshire	6a
Somersetshire	X,XI	Somersetshire	5c
Staffordshire	XVI,XVII,XVIII	Staffordshire	6b
Suffolk	XIV,XII,XIII	Suffolk	4a,3b
Surrey	IV	Surrey	2a,1d
Sussex	VII	Sussex	2b
Warwickshire	XXV	Warwickshire	6b,6c,6d
Westmorland	XXV	Westmorland	10b
Wiltshire	VIII	Wiltshire	5a
Worcestershire	XVIII	Worcestershire	6b,6c
Yorkshire	XXI,XXII,XXIII,XXIV	Yorkshire	9a,9b,9c,9d

Regnal Years

TUDORS

Henry VII	1485-1509 (aged 52 yrs)	Roman Catholic
Henry VIII	1509-1547 (aged 56 yrs)	Roman Catholic until 1534 when he became Head of the English Church
Edward VI	1547-1553 (aged 16 yrs)	Church of England
(Lady Jane Grey	1553-1553 (aged 17 yrs)	Church of England
Reigned 9 days — executed 1554)		
Mary I	1553-1558 (aged 42 yrs)	Roman Catholic
Elizabeth I	1558-1603 (aged 69 yrs)	Church of England

STUARTS

James I	1603-1625 (aged 59 yrs)	Church of England
(also James VI of Scotland)		
Charles I	1625-1649 (aged 49 yrs)	Church of England
(beheaded)		

COMMONWEALTH (INTERREGNUM)
(declared 19 May 1649)

Oliver Cromwell	1653-1658 (aged 59 yrs)	Protestant—Puritan
(Lord Protector)		
Richard Cromwell	1658-1659	Protestant—Puritan
(Lord Protector)		
(son of Oliver Cromwell, lived until 1712)		

RESTORATION OF THE STUARTS

Charles II	1660-1685 (aged 55 yrs)	Church of England
(his regnal years are calculated from death of his father in 1649)		
James II	1685-1688 (deposed)	Roman Catholic
(also James VII of Scotland — died in exile in 1701)		

INTERREGNUM
(December 11 1688 to February 13 1689)

William III and	1689-1702 (aged 51 yrs)	Church of England
Mary II	1689-1694 (aged 32 yrs)	Church of England
Anne	1702-1714 (aged 49 yrs)	Church of England

HOUSE OF HANOVER

George I	1714-1727 (aged 67 yrs)	Church of England
George II	1727-1760 (aged 77 yrs)	Church of England
George III	1760-1820 (aged 81 yrs)	Church of England
George IV	1820-1830 (aged 68 yrs)	Church of England
William IV	1830-1837 (aged 71 yrs)	Church of England
Victoria	1837-1901 (aged 81 yrs)	Church of England

HOUSE OF SAXE-COBURG

| Edward VII | 1901-1910 (aged 68 yrs) | Church of England |

HOUSE OF WINDSOR

George V	1910-1936 (aged 70 yrs)	Church of England
Edward VIII	1936 (abdicated after 325 days)	Church of England
George VI	1936-1952 (aged 56 yrs)	Church of England
Elizabeth II	1952-	Church of England

Regnal years were calculated from the date of accession of the monarch until the date of death.

Useful addresses

Baptist Union Library, The Angus Library, Regent's Park College, Oxford, OX1 2LB.

Baptist Union of Scotland, Baptist Church House, 14 Aytown Road, Pollokshields, Glasgow, G41 5RT.

Baptist Union of Wales, Ilston House, 94 Mansell Street, Swansea, SA1 5TU.

British Library and Dept of Manuscripts, Great Russell St. London, WC1B 3DG.

College of Arms, Queen Victoria Street, London, EC4U 4BT.

Commonwealth War Graves Commission, 3 Marlow Road, Maidenhead, Berks, SL6 7DX.

Court of Session, Parliament Square, Edinburgh.

General Registry, Finch Road, Douglas, Isle of Man.

House of Lords Record Office, House of Lords, London, SW1A 0AW

Huguenot Society of London, of Great Britain and Ireland, The Huguenot Library University College, Gower Street, London, WC1E 6BT.

Imperial War Museum and Dept of Documents, Lambeth Road, London, SE1 6HZ.

India Office, Library and Records, Orbit House, Blackfriars Road, London, SE1.

Institute of Agricultural History and Museum of English, Rural Life, University of Reading, Whiteknights, Reading, Berks, RG6 2AG.

John Rylands University Library of Manchester, Methodist Archives and Research Centre, Deansgate, Manchester, M13 9PL.

Judicial Greffe, States Building, Royal Square, St. Helier, Jersey, Channel Islands.

Lambeth Palace Library, London, SE1 7JU.

Manx Museum Library, Kingswood Grove, Douglas, Isle of Man.

Metropolitan Police Historical Museum, Bow Street Police Station, London, WC2.

Ministry of Defence, Army Medal Office, Government Office Buildings, Droitwich, Worcs., WR9 8AU.

Ministry of Defence, Bourne Avenue, Hayes, Middlesex.

Mocatta Library, University College of London, Gower Street, London,WC1E 6BT.

Museum of the History of Education, The University of Leeds, Leeds, W. Yorks.

National Library of Scotland, George IV Bridge, Edinburgh, EH1 1EW.

National Library of Ireland, Kildare Street, Dublin 1.

National Museum of Labour History, Limehouse Town Hall, Commercial Road, London, E14.

National Register of Archives (Scotland), General Register House, Edinburgh, EH1 3YY.

Post Office Archives, Post Office Headquarters Buildings, St. Martin's Le Grand, London, EC1A 1HR.

Public Record Office of Ireland, Four Courts, Dublin, 7.

RAF Personnel Management Centre, Eastern Avenue, Barnwood, Gloucester.

Royal Commission on Historical Manuscripts (also National Register of Archives), Quality House, Quality Court, Chancery Lane, London WC2A 1HP.

Royal Marines Museum, Royal Marines, Eastney, Southampton, Hants PO4 9PX.

Shetland Archives, 44 King Harald Street, Lerwick, ZE1 OEQ.

Theatre Museum, 1E Tavistock Street, Covent Garden, London WC2 7PA.

The Divorce Registry, Somerset House, Strand, London, WC2R 1LP.

The Greffe, The Royal Court House, St Peter Port, Guernsey, Channel Islands.

Welsh Folk Museum, St Fagans, Cardiff, CF5 6XR.

Westminster Diocesan Archives, Archbishops House, Ambrosden Avenue, London, SW1 1QJ.

The Generation Grid

The Generation Grid was composed by Mr F. Leeson, Editor of the Society of Genealogist magazine, *Leesons Letter's* as they are sometimes known, are now quite widely used.

Genealogists frequently allot letters or numbers to successive generations in pedigrees, in order to facilitate reference to them or to identify individuals: but many of these private systems have the serious drawback that they lack a common 'datum line' and are not 'open-ended'. In the case of single-surname studies, where pedigrees covering different family groups, or branches all bearing the same surname — and often the same forename — occur, the need for a standard system, which can also be used, after county or parish divisions, as a means of filing slips, becomes vital.

A system of allotting identifying letters to each 330-year span of time from

AD 1380 (beyond which few average pedigrees stretch) to AD 2159 has been devized by the Surname Archive for the purpose of separating and grouping the generations, and the originators hope that, by becoming more generally known, the 'generation letter' may become a standard reference in genealogy

The arbitrary 'datum line of this system is the S (for self) generation, representing those of us now in full maturity and, incidentally, the large post-World War 1 generation of the 1920s. Similarly, T generation represents the post World War II progeny of the 1950s.

The full list is set out below for convenience and it will be noted that there are useful mnemonics in that E introduces the 'Elizabethan' century of the 1500s and the O was allocated to the 'Double-O' generation of the 1800s.

In those rare instances where pedigrees stretch back before 1380, a letter preceded by a minus sign may be used, working backward from Z; thus an ancestor born between 1290 and 1319 would be a X generation person.

Apart from purposes of identification, a number of other obvious uses come to mind for the Generation Grid; it can be placed over old charts (e.g. Visitation pedigrees) where perhaps there is only one dating clue, and generations coming before or after this 'datum line' can be read off and compared with similarly-labelled clues in other records; or in lists of marriages or burials one may make provisional assumptions about the subjects, for filing and other purposes, by saying that the former represent persons of the previous generation letter, and the latter of two generations previous — e.g. a burial without a given age in 1870 would be labelled Generation O, and a marriage in 1870 Generation P.

NB: Two letters together may be used where it is necessary to stretch, telescope, or otherwise adjust 'out-of-step' generation — e.g. stretching +A, AB, B, BC, D, etc; telescoping +A, BC, D, etc.

A	1380-1409	N	1770-1799
B	1410-1439	O	1800-1829
C	1440-1469	P	1830-1859
D	1470-1499	Q	1860-1889
E	1500-1529	R	1890-1919
F	1530-1559	S	1920-1949
G	1560-1589	T	1950-1979
H	1590-1619	U	1980-2009
I	1620-1649	V	2010-2039
J	1650-1679	W	2040-2069
K	1680-1709	X	2070-2099
L	1710-1739	Y	2100-2129
M	1740-1769	Z	2130-2159

INDEX

Law Amendment Act, 106, 114,
    116
Population England/Wales, 40
Praedial Tithe, 100
Presbyterians, 71, 76
Principal,
    Probate Registry, 84, 87, 88
    Registry, Family Division, 88
Printed word, 155
Printing presses, 121
Prison Registers, 77
Prisoners of War, 154
Prisons, 127, 154
Probate, 88
    Act, 80
    Jurisdictions, 79, 86
    Records, 168
Protestantism, 70
Protestation Oath Returns, 49
Public Record Office of Northern
    Ireland, 173
Public Schools, 154
Puritans, 71

Quakers, 61, 71, 76
Quarter Session,
    Records, 92, 116, 121, 122
    Rolls, 120, 121, 126

RAF, 34, 169
    Museum, 174
Ragged schools, 154
Recognizances, 120
Record Measures Act, 54
Recording information, 22
Recruitment, Army, 122
Rector, 99
Recusant Rolls, 48, 61
Reference Library, 52
Register,
    of Corrected Entries (RCE), 35
    Office, 26
    Registrar, 26
Registration,
    District Reference Numbers,
        199
    of Companies, 169
Removal Certificates, 103, 104
Removals, 124, 154
Right of Burial Grant, 21
Rogues, 110
Rose Act, 64
Rotton, Major, 12
Royal,
    Air Force Returns, 34
    Air Force Museum, 145
    Artillery, 144
    Navy, 163, 166, 168, 169
    Warrant Holders, 167
Rural District Councils, 126

Sacrament Certificates, 121
Sale of Indulgences, 70
Salisbury, Wiltshire, 111
School(s), 126, 154
    admission records, 102
    Board, 126
    Church, 126
    local, 126

prizes, 21
reports, 21
Sunday, 126
Schoolmasters, licencing of, 128
Scottish,
    Censuses, 45
    Civil Registration, 35
    Record Office, 174
    Wills, 85
Secretary Hand, 159
Seisin/Seizin, 138
Separation, 128, 147
Sephardic Jews, 77
Serf, 134
Service,
    Dept Registers, 36
    Records (Scotland), 36
Settlement
    Certificates, 103, 104
    Examinations 1850, 103
    Law of, 106
Shipping, 166
    and Seamen's Records, 34
Shipwrecks, 169
Slander, 128
Soldiers, 122
South Yorkshire, 89
Specialist Collections, 170
Speenhamland system, 114
Staffordshire, 89
Stamp,
    Act of 1813, 84
    Act of 1783, 64
    Duty Act, 69
Statute,
    of Appeals, 147
    of Enrollments, 146
Steward, 135
Stonewarden, 98
Strays, 154
Suffolk, 89
Suit, 138
Sunday School,
    prizes, 20
    registers, 102
Superintendent Registrars, 72
Supreme Court of Judicature, 147
Surgeons, Licencing of, 128
Surrenders, 135
Surveyors of the Highways, 98
Sussex East, 89
Swedenborgian Church, 76

Tail, 138
Tailor, 59
Tax Records, 47, 169
Taxes, 127
Teachers, unlicenced, 128
Test Act 1672, 121
Testament, 80
Testamentary Causes, 127
Testator, 80
Tetbury Workhouse Circular 1799,
    117
Thirty-nine Articles, 71
Times, The, 142
Tithes, 99, 100, 151, 168
Tiverton, Devon, 90
Toleration Act, 72

Toll Houses, 122
Tolpuddle, 139
Tontines, 157
Trade Union Records, 21
Trademarks, 168
Transfers, 135
Transport Records, 168
Transportation, 154
    of Felons, 121
Treason, 136
Trespass, 137
Turnpikes, 122
Tyne and Wear, 89

UK High Commission Deaths, 34
Unitarian Church, 71, 76
United Reform Church, 74, 76
    History Society, 174
Unity of Bretheren, 76
Universities, 154
Unlawful Socities Act 1799, 121
Urban Councils, 126
Useful dates, 195

Vagabonds, 110
Vagrancy, 109, 110
Verbal Wills, 80
Vestry, 93
    Minutes, 94
Vicar, 99
Vicar's Warden, 94
Victuals, corrupt, 136
Villein, 134

War,
    Deaths, 34
    Graves Commission, 144
    Office (WO), 163, 164
    Registers from 1899 (Scotland), 36
    Revenue Act, 49
Warminster Union — Outdoor Relief
    1859, 115
Watercourses, 137
Waywarden, 98
Weights and Measures, 136
Wells, Mary, 111
Welsh Wills, 85
Wesley,
    Charles, 75
    Indian Colonies, 167
    Midlands, 89
Will(s), 79, 80, 126
    Abstracts, 86
    Act 1836/7, 81
    after 1858, 87
    and Admons, 127
    Disputes, 127
    Inland Revenue, 83
    Nuncupative, 81
    of John Little of Wroughton 1728,
        81
    Statute of, 82
Workhouse(s), 114, 122, 124
    Master, 116
    System, 116
    Union, 126
World War II, 36

Young, Brigham, 131